DANCING BETWEEN THE RAINDROPS

A DAUGHTER'S REFLECTIONS ON LOVE AND LOSS

Also by Lisa Braxton

The Talking Drum

Dancing Between the Raindrops: A Daughter's Reflections on Love and Loss

Published 2024 by Sea Crow Press
Barnstable, MA
www.seacrowpress.com

Paperback ISBN: 978-1-961864-08-5
Ebook ISBN: 978-1-961864-09-2
Library of Congress Control Number: 2024933100

In memory of Mom and Dad:
Elizabeth Williams Braxton
December 14, 1936-October 19, 2020
Julian V. Braxton
September 10, 1932-September 20, 2022

DANCING BETWEEN THE RAINDROPS

A DAUGHTER'S REFLECTIONS ON LOVE AND LOSS

LISA BRAXTON

Sea Crow Press

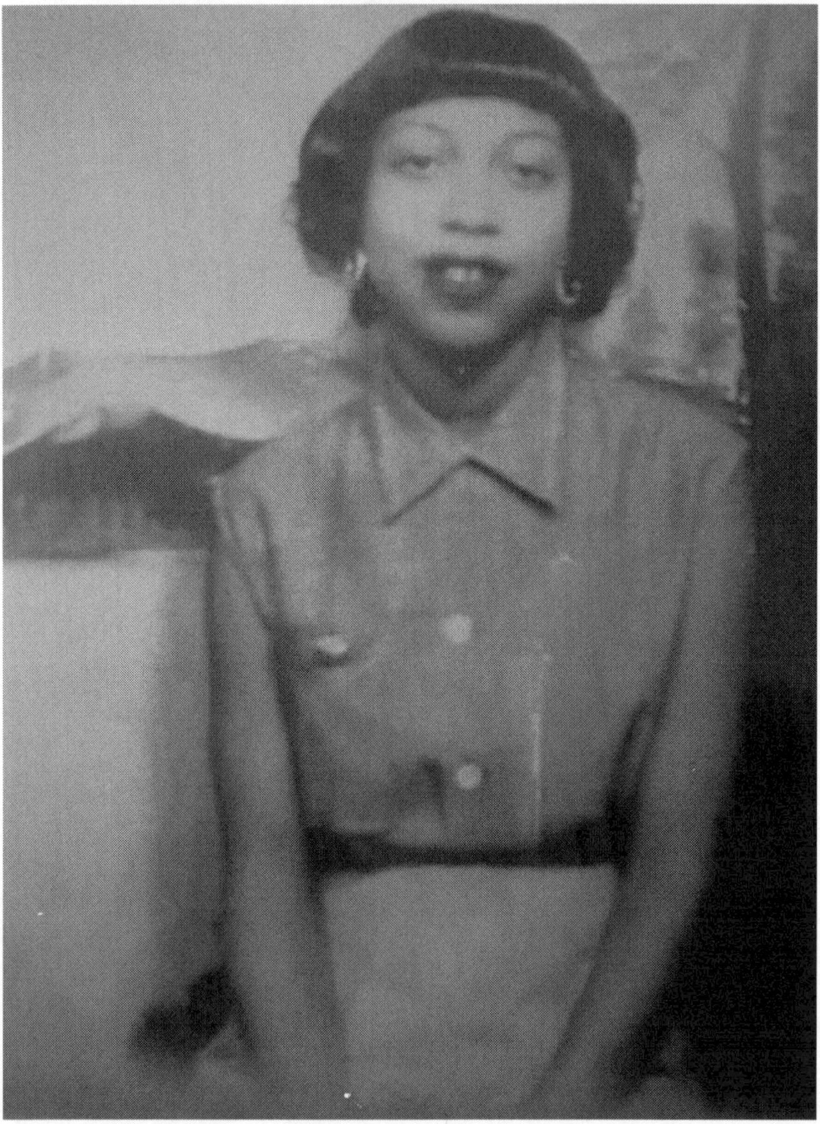

Chapter 1
Soothing a Broken Heart

Mom wanted to be a writer. To put her creativity on paper and share it with the world. When I was a little girl, she showed me a fragment of a story she had started, a semi-autobiographical piece about a young married woman who had a tough childhood and is excited to learn that her nausea is caused by morning sickness. She can't wait until her husband comes home from work to tell him that she is pregnant with their first child.

"That's really good, Mommy," I remember saying. "You should finish it."

Mom gave me a sideways glance and shook her head. "I don't think it's any good."

I reassured her that it was, that I wanted to read more. But she put the story away.

Years later, after my sister, Sylvia, was born, Mom agreed to support my father's dream of opening a clothing store. She invested savings in it, designed a business plan, taught my father how to use a sewing machine and make alterations, helped him choose merchandise, waited on customers, and rang up sales. All while taking care of my sister and me. During those years and later, she'd sprinkle conversations with talk of being a writer, wistfulness in her voice.

She never failed to tell me how proud she was when she read the bylined stories I wrote while on a college internship at the hometown newspaper and after I graduated for a major metropolitan newspaper. When I sent her links to short stories I'd gotten published in literary magazines, she'd say, "One day I'm going to write my memoirs."

She had plenty of stories to tell. She shared many of them with me: growing up poor in Virginia's Shenandoah Valley in the 1940s and '50s under the Jim Crow era's form of segregation; pushing a white playmate into a pond when the child stated firmly that black people were inferior; tugging on her mother's sleeve and asking why they had to stand in the back of the bus when there were plenty of empty seats up front and being told, "Hush up, child!". How her biological father, a prominent medical doctor in the community, refused to acknowledge her, the result of a brief relationship he'd had with my grandmother. How her stepfather burned down their rental home and put her family on the run from the authorities, hiding out in abandoned houses and sleeping on cardboard. How she'd moved as an 18-year-old newlywed from her small Virginia community to a bustling New England factory city.

Sylvia and I would give Mom blank books to encourage her to write. I'd tell her about writing classes she could take at nearby writing centers and community colleges, but she'd always find reasons not to enroll.

Then, one day when she was in her late 70s she called me to vent about her disappointments, how she'd spent so many years - decades in fact - supporting my father's dream, and how she wanted something of her own. I mentioned an online creative nonfiction class I was taking and how encouraging the instructor was. To my surprise, Mom had me send her the link to the writing center's website. I walked her through the online registration process.

Each week Mom wrote a scene about her childhood, many of the stories she had told me and some I hadn't heard before. After the course had ended, she printed copies of her work and proudly showed them to my sister and me. Then she tucked the writing away.

When Mom was diagnosed with late-stage ovarian cancer, I was devastated. I had to remind myself to breathe. I lost interest in food and dropped 20 pounds. I didn't want to face the prospect that my biggest champion would no longer be by my side.

Months after Mom's surgeries and chemo treatments, doctors told us there was nothing more they could do for her. Mom had mere weeks to live. My sister and I returned home and moved into the bedroom with her and gave her 24-hour care. We were with her when she took her last breath.

As we grieved, we busied ourselves sorting through Mom's personal effects. We spent hours cleaning out her desk. It was her special place where she made phone calls, paid bills, wrote letters and filed away important documents. On her desktop computer she'd keep up with email correspondence, play the occasional game of solitaire, and smile proudly at her grandchildren displayed in pictures on the desktop slideshow.

In one of the desk's cubby holes we came across a stack of papers. Within the stack were two letters, one addressed to me and one addressed to my sister, written in blue ballpoint pen in my mother's beautiful cursive handwriting. Time stopped for me as I read her words:

Dear Lisa,
Words can never express my love for you. You are my first born whom I love with all my heart. As a child, I felt unloved and have felt that way most of my life. But I know that you and Sylvia love me and that has sustained me. I wish you nothing but happiness.
Love,
Mom

In my mind I heard my mother's voice saying the words as I read them. I imagined the joy and heartache she felt as she penned them.

I dream about my mother often. In one of my dreams, we're on our way out the door to the shopping mall. Mom is in her late 30s, full of life, ready to catch some sales in both the department stores and the boutiques, and I'm a teenager, anticipating what Mom will buy for me. When I wake up from that dream and others like it, I feel hollow, remembering that Mom is gone and the dreams are only a momentary break from reality.

Then I think about her letter. Her words comfort me as the tears come.

Mom didn't become the writer she dreamed of. She never saw her words printed in a bound publication placed on the shelf of a bookstore or showcased on the homepage of an online book retailer. But she became something much more extraordinary. She became the author that I needed, the writer of powerful words that soothe my broken heart.

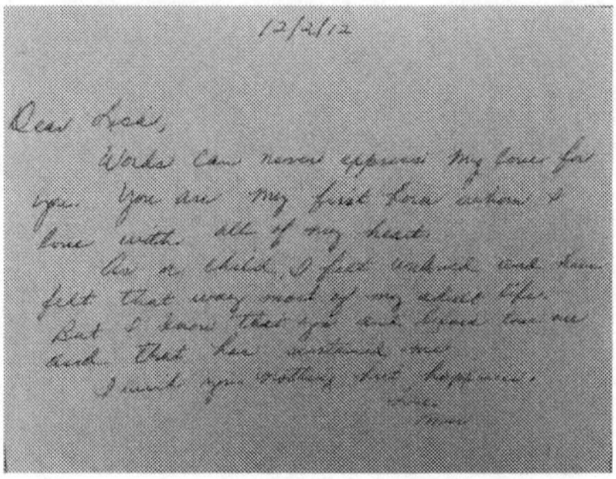
12/2/12

Dear Lisa,

Words can never express my love for you. You are my first love whom I love with all of my heart.

As a child, I felt unloved and have felt that way most of my adult life. But I know that you and [illegible] love me and that has sustained me.

I wish you nothing but happiness.

Love,
Mom

Chapter 2
Revolver

It is 20 degrees Fahrenheit. I am visiting my parents in southern Connecticut for the weekend as are my sister and brother-in-law, Sylvia and Aron. Mom and Dad think it's a social visit. We don't let them know that we're here to try to find a loaded revolver in their backyard.

As the sun rises the three of us meet in the kitchen in our hats, gloves, boots and heavy coats. I carefully slip the key into the bolt lock of the back door and turn it, hoping not to wake Mom and Dad. Dad's not that much of a concern. At age 83 he's lost most of his hearing. Mom's another story. She's always been a light sleeper. We manage to get out the door without either of them stirring.

Our boots crunch through the layer of icy snow in the backyard. Sylvia and Aron head for the shed at the far end of the yard. I peel off from the others to check things out in the carport.

The carport is a reflection of Dad's frailty and gradually deepening dementia. It's one of his recent "home improvements." Made out of scrap wood, it's an eyesore. An open carport with a flat roof, it has the look of a gigantic coffee table in need of shellacking.

Their SUV barely fits, allowing about an inch of clearance for the roof. If Dad ran over a large enough pebble, he'd be looking at getting a new paint job for the vehicle. If you didn't park just right, getting out of the drivers' side would require the skill of a contortionist. To avoid banging the doors into support beams on the sides meant slithering out.

I squeeze past a three foot by five-foot bow window propped up on a slab of wood near the grill of the SUV. The living room of Mom and Dad's Cape Cod-style house has a bay window and it's in good condition. However, Dad said he felt a bow window would be an improvement, so he bought one. It's been sitting in the driveway ever since.

Behind the bow window, fixtures from the clothing store Mom and Dad owned and operated for 40 years populate the rest of the carport - a circular rack that once held dozens of pairs of men's bell bottoms, plastic male mannequin legs that showcased slacks in the store's display window, a large black cabinet where platform shoes were displayed.

Inside the drawers of the cabinet was overstock - gabardine sweaters, wide neckties, bottles of musk cologne, cufflinks.

As I yank open the top drawer, somewhere between 40-50 rusted door knobs roll around like marbles. They are the supply Dad drew from to replace knobs on doors of rental properties they used to own.

I pull open the equally stubborn bottom drawer to discover Dad's yellowed copies of the Connecticut and New York City newspapers from 1963 with screaming headlines in giant font announcing the assassination of John. F. Kennedy.

"These are collector's items," Dad had said in recent months, a gleam in his eyes as he held the "extra" editions in his fist. "They'll be worth something someday."

No sign of the revolver.

Leaving the carport, I head in the direction of the makeshift shed Dad had built at the far end of the backyard to store additional store fixtures, paperwork and clothing stock - inventory he couldn't part with once the business closed down. Mom had Dad also made room for toys my niece and nephew played with when they were little. When I walk in, I find Sylvia and Aron frantically rifling through papers, emptying shoeboxes, yanking open file cabinet drawers, pushing aside mannequins and tie racks.

"Your father's got a gun in the shed." Mom let this remark slip out during a phone conversation I had with her as I was about to leave the office and head home.

"He pulled it out once and pointed it in the distance and told me, 'If anyone breaks into the house, just pull the trigger.' Then he put the gun away. But I'm not gonna use it." Her voice became shrill as it often did when she became emotional. "I wouldn't go near that thing. I wouldn't even look at it."

I was having a hard time absorbing what she was saying. I couldn't fathom my father having a gun after all these years nor giving my mother a do-it-yourself firearms lesson.

"Are you saying that there's a loaded gun in the shed?" I could hear my own voice becoming shrill.

A pregnant pause.

"Don't worry about it. I'm not gonna use it. I'm not gonna touch it."

I had a flashback to a day in the early 1970s when I was nine or ten years old. The clothing store had only been in operation a few years. I was at the store after school when I noticed a revolver on a shelf below the cash register. My mother said my father had it there for protection. Could that be the very same gun in Mom and Dad's backyard all these years later?

"So exactly where is it in the shed, Mom?"

"Oh, I shouldn't have said anything. I shouldn't have told you. Maybe it's not in the shed. Maybe your father moved it somewhere else. Stop worrying. I shouldn't have told you."

I continued to push for more details. My mother continued to retreat.

I sent an urgent text to my sister. She texted back immediately and said that on a visit months earlier my 13-year-old niece had been playing in the shed. She'd discovered an old dollhouse and was in there for a good hour. We agreed to meet in Connecticut, find the gun and dispose of it.

Sylvia and Aron's search is also in vain. I decide to retrace their search in case they missed something. They did. I find the revolver in the top drawer of a file cabinet under a pile of papers. All those detective shows I watched growing up pay off. I put my winter gloves back on before handling the gun to make sure my prints aren't on it.

In preparation for our "reunion" visit to Mom and Dad I'd ordered a gun case. It is cushioned to hold a gun in place and has a combination lock to secure it even further. The three of us look at each other, not knowing what next step to take. If we call the police, they might arrive armed and ready to shoot. We'd read too many stories in the media about African Americans wrongfully shot by police and killed or brutally injured to take that risk. Also, they could arrest us or Dad. He's in his 80s, but we don't want to take that risk either. We don't want to drive it to the police station. What if we get stopped for a broken taillight or passing into a lane without signaling? They'd inspect the car and we'd be arrested.

We decide to dump the case in the bottom of the general trash barrel behind the shed, figuring that on trash day Dad will pull the barrel to the curb and that will be the end of it. The three of us pull trash out of the recycling trash barrel and pile it on top of the gun case. We close the lid and return to the house.

About a week and a half later I call Mom before I leave work and casually weave the trash pickup into the conversation, asking if Dad pulled the barrels in front of the house.

"Your father says the cans are too heavy."

My heart drops into my stomach. "He says *what*?"

"They're too full. They're too heavy for him to pull out front."

"What's he going to do?" I do all I can to keep my voice measured.

"I don't know. That's up to him."

We are quiet for a while. Then she continues. "There's a man down the street who helps out sometimes. Maybe we can get him to pull them around."

I say a silent prayer that he's willing to do it.

"Yes, Mom. That's a good idea. A real good idea."

Chapter 3
Welcome to the Neighborhood

They stepped out of front doors, proceeded down spacious brick pathways to the foot of their manicured lawns, and with the precision of a military unit, pivoted to face us. All of them were white men and women - homeowners in a leafy Fairfield County, Connecticut enclave anchored by raised ranches, Dutch Colonials and split-level homes.

All eyes were on us - my mother, father, sister, and me - as the realtor led us down the front steps of a well-appointed three-bedroom, three-bathroom house with a two-car garage that she'd just shown us.

It was around 1969. I was eight or nine years old at the time. My dad was carrying my sister, who was a toddler wearing diaper pants. I remember my parents' stride toward our car slowed as they realized that we were under surveillance. The members of our "audience," consisting of about a dozen people on both sides of the street, were expressionless, motionless, arms hanging at their sides. Their body language was unreadable but their presence screamed volumes.

I don't recall what the realtor said to my parents as she took in the scene, but I remember that she was flustered, apologetic, and tripped over her words. It was a moment that she had apparently not anticipated—the visceral reaction of white residents to a black family being shown a house in their affluent neighborhood. At my age I didn't think deeply about their demonstration, but I did find it odd that all of those adults were standing on their front lawns, their eyes on us. As my father put our car into gear, I scooted to the edge of my seat in the back to eavesdrop on my parents' conversation as I often did when we were on car rides.

My mother leaned toward my father, and in a hushed tone said, "They don't want us living here." After a moment, he gave a slight nod and said just as quietly, "I know." I slid back on my seat, my eavesdropping undetected.

At that age I knew a little bit about prejudice. I had a classmate who made a remark when we were in the third grade that stunned me. My class was lined up at the water fountain after coming back from chapel at the church next door that operated our parochial school. She blurted out angrily, "I wish all the black people would go back to Africa!" When I came home upset about the incident my parents sat me down for a talk and said that most likely she'd heard that remark from her parents and was repeating what they'd said.

A little girl in my neighborhood with whom I'd spent countless hours having pretend picnics and competing to swing the highest on my swing set made the statement one day as we played near the fence that divided our yards, "White people are better than black people." With indignation I retorted, "No, they're not!" My naïve childhood self didn't understand why anyone would think something so ridiculous. I felt that the idea of white people being better than black people turned logic on its head. How could one group be better than another?

After we ping ponged our positions on the matter for a while, I ran into the house to tell my mother about my friend's unfathomable pronouncement. I still remember the pained look on my mother's face.

"You're not playing with her anymore," Mom shouted.

"But why?"

For Mom, the subject was closed.

I knew my friend was wrong, but I saw no reason to end the

friendship. Soon enough my friend and I were playing together as we had before. Mom didn't object.

At the time of the silent front lawn protest, I didn't know that this was but the latest racial indignity my parents had had shoved in their faces. They came of age in the early 1950s in the western section of Virginia in the Shenandoah Valley. This region is known generally for its picturesque, bucolic nature, but also for an ugliness manifested in hostility for many African Americans.

Because of Jim Crow laws, my parents attended segregated schools. They told me that whenever they came close to approaching a white person on the sidewalk, they had to lower their heads and step into the street. Taking a bus involved going to the "black" section in the back and standing if there were no seats, even if there were empty seats up front. Dining out involved going to the back door of a restaurant for takeout. My mother recounts saying nothing for fear of reprisal when white individuals would cut in front of her in store checkout lines And when she did get to the front of the line, she'd count her change to make sure she wasn't being cheated.

My parents shared these accounts with me and, later, with my sister when she was old enough to understand because they wanted us to have the best life possible. They wanted us to advocate for ourselves and understand that people would not always have our best interests in mind. They didn't want us to be held back by people who used race as a means of control and disrespect.

Both of my parents knew that because of the racial climate, growing up poor in the South with only high school educations and not having connections to anyone with any level of power or influence, their prospects would be limited if they stayed in Virginia. Like a massive number of African Americans from southern rural areas during the middle of the past century, they made their way North. For my parents, "The Promised Land" was Bridgeport, Connecticut, an industrial force at the time.

Once they'd arrived, they realized that they hadn't escaped racism, but encountered a subtler form of it. My mother would respond over the phone to a classified ad for an employment opportunity, be encouraged to come to the location to fill out an application, and then be told once she walked in the door that the job had been filled.

My parents discovered that there were only certain apartment buildings in the city that would rent to them and moved into one housing African American and Latinx renters. When they purchased their Cape Cod-style home in early 1961, they were the only non-white family on their block in the working-class neighborhood. A neighbor later told my mother that after she and my father bought the house, a man who lived around the corner from them went to every house on the block and "warned" them that a black family was moving in. She was told that one family put their house on the market in response and moved to the suburbs. It was common knowledge that at least one property owner, in possession of a large parcel of land in the neighborhood, would not sell homes to African Americans.

By the time my parents looked at that house in suburbia - one of many like it they were shown during that period of time - my father had moved up from being a machinist at the General Electric plant in Bridgeport to being foreman. My parents were opening up a business, a high-fashion men's clothing store. They had me enrolled at the parochial school and my mother was considering pursuing a bachelor's degree and possibly law school. Mom and Dad were invited to join some of the African American professional, charitable and civic clubs and organizations in Bridgeport. Moving out of their starter home to suburbia seemed like a logical step.

However, after much discussion, my parents chose not to pursue that house. They were concerned about hostility from the neighbors in light of the demonstration. Later, Mom told me they worried about my sister and me being subjected to racial taunts and remarks from neighborhood kids and classmates and also thought we'd feel isolated.

Every so often on car rides near that neighborhood, I'd overhear my mother, her voice catching in her throat, go back to that day and say to my father how terrible it was for "those people to come out onto their front lawns like that."

Mom and Dad stopped looking at houses and made improvements to our Cape Cod-style home. They had the roof raised on the back and the attic upgraded so my sister and I could have separate bedrooms and poured the money they had set aside for a house into the clothing store.

Nonetheless, they continued for years talking off and on about moving. Mom especially wanted to upgrade. She wanted a house where she could feel proud to entertain, reflecting their station in life. It never happened.

By the time I reached my early teens, I noticed significant changes in the neighborhood. My white playmates had moved away. The white families whose homes flanked ours were gone. I heard that the property owner who refused to sell to African Americans had passed away. The neighborhood became more African American and Latinx. Recent immigrants moved in. A dramatic level of white flight occurred not just in my neighborhood but throughout the city. The white families most likely moved to the town where my parents had gone house hunting all those years earlier or to another Fairfield County suburb.

In 1958, political scientist Morton Grodzins identified that "once the proportion of non-whites exceeds the limits of the neighborhood's tolerance for interracial living, whites move out." Grodzins termed this phenomenon the tipping point in the study of white flight, the sudden or gradual large-scale migration of white people from areas becoming more racially or ethnoculturally diverse. Economists attribute white flight both to racism and economics.

In the 1960s and '70s "There goes the neighborhood" became a popular catchphrase, most likely originating as an expression of concern by a homeowner that a newcomer would lower property values and, in many instances, an expression of fear among white homeowners when the first minority family moved in.

Undoubtedly, the thought of property values deteriorating was on the minds of the silent activists when we visited their neighborhood. Some of those residents may have lived in a Bridgeport neighborhood at one time and escaped to the suburbs when the racial ratio reached the tipping point. Our presence may have symbolized a nipping at their heels when they thought they had outrun us.

Black flight is a term applied to the migration of African Americans from predominantly black or mixed inner-city areas to suburbs and newly constructed homes on the outer edges of cities. In some ways their goals have been similar to those of the white middle class heading to the suburbs: newer housing, better schools for their children, and attractive environments. Just what my parents had in mind in their house hunting.

I couldn't help but think back to that "front lawn moment" in the mid-1990s when I had a realtor help me look for an apartment in the coal region of Northeastern Pennsylvania. I had accepted a television news reporter position there and had driven to the area ahead of my start date for a weekend hoping to secure an apartment. Toward the end of the Saturday, after not finding anything I liked, the realtor suggested that I look at an apartment that was in her building. It was a charming corner unit in the heart of the downtown and had large, old-fashioned windows that let in plenty of light, decorative moldings along the doorways and ceilings, and walls of mirrors that had me reminiscing about visiting the Hall of Mirrors at the Palace of Versailles when I was a high school exchange student. The apartment was less than a block from the TV station. I'd be able to walk to work, the bank, the library, church, and just about everywhere else. I knew the moment I walked in the door that I wanted to rent it.

The realtor got on the phone with the owner to let him know that she had a renter. I noticed her jaw tighten in reaction to whatever he was saying on the other end. She glanced at me and said a series of "No"s into the receiver. I knew what was going on and was incensed. He was asking her about race. She next responded to him with a "Yes." Then after a pause, she said, "If you won't rent to her, she'll do an investigative report on you." When she hung up, her tone was apologetic. She stated that some people in the community were narrow minded. She added that the owner wanted to meet with me before deciding whether or not to rent the apartment.

I looked forward to it. I wanted to meet this man who decided that because of race I shouldn't be rented the apartment and only reconsidered under threat. After my meeting with him, the realtor handed me a rental agreement. I had mixed feelings as I signed and dated the document, but the window of time for me to find another apartment was limited.

Sociologists are finding that as more people of color are moving into the suburbs, white flight is happening all over again. Samuel Kye at Indiana University has documented an exodus of white residents as more minorities have entered the middle class and established themselves in healthy suburban neighborhoods. Kye discovered that white flight was particularly pronounced in areas with fewer high school dropouts, strong home values, median income levels, and large numbers of professionals. Low-income whites didn't have the means to leave. His conclusions are in line with those of other academics who've done similar research.

The expression, "There goes the neighborhood," may have gone out of fashion decades ago, but the mindset persists, in spite of all of the conversations this nation has had in recent years about race through town hall meetings, academic forums, college classes, debates, discussions, special reports in the media, speeches by politicians, lawsuits, and informal talks among friends and colleagues.

Of course, blame for Mom and Dad never moving can't be entirely placed on their reaction to the silent protest of the homeowners in the leafy Fairfield County enclave, but I'm sure it played some part.

A few months before Mom passed away, during one of her hospitalizations, I overheard Dad - suffering from significant hearing loss and dementia - on speakerphone with a realtor asking to be shown a particular house in suburbia. It had four bedrooms, three bathrooms and a two car garage. The realtor responded by reminding him that he and Mom had previously stated in the past year or so that they were not looking. After he hung up, he came to Sylvia and me and pleaded with us to buy the house for Mom. My heart was breaking.

In the early days of Mom's home hospice, I played gospel music for her, the style she sang in the Baptist church of her childhood and heard from the revivalists who came through her community. She enjoyed the music I played for her, rocking her head from side-to-side and smiling as she rested in bed. Not long before her death I decided to play the same selections for her even though she hadn't talked in days and seemed to be unconscious. I thought on some level it might be soothing.

Mom began to cry, something I didn't expect. Then her crying became sobs. I didn't know what to do. I thought about turning the music off, but decided to let it play, thinking that maybe she needed to express her emotions. I couldn't help but wonder if she was sobbing because she was aware that she was dying in the same bedroom that she and Dad first occupied in 1961, that she never got the dream house that she wanted.

What we as a family experienced all those years ago during that house hunt was a moment I didn't fully understand at the time but never forgot. Mom and Dad never forgot either. Racism and bias took up residence in our family. It is unfortunate that it did.

Chapter 4
The World I Didn't Know Existed

I was a painfully shy child growing up in Connecticut in the late 1960s. I preferred sitting in my mother's lap as she watched her afternoon soap operas to going outside to play. When it came time to enroll me in kindergarten, my parents weren't sure public school would be right for me. They were concerned that because of the large class sizes, I would retreat further into my cocoon. They decided to enroll me in a private, parochial elementary school with grades Kindergarten through Eighth.

I remember my mother dressing me in a brand new plaid jumper, color-coordinated knee socks, and Buster Brown shoes that first day and leading me by the hand to my classroom in the little brick building. I climbed onto my seat and found comfort in the friendly faces that surrounded me. Class sizes were small. I gradually formed friendships. After a few weeks I was raising my hand freely and was playfully called the teacher's pet.

We began each day with devotion and religion. Wednesdays we walked over to the church for chapel. One Wednesday, when I was in the third grade, we children made our usual stop at the water fountain after leaving the church. Over the sound of chattering, one of my classmates blurted out in an angry voice, "I wish all the black people would go back to Africa!"

All conversation stopped. A hush fell over the line of students as her words lingered in the air. I instinctively searched the faces of the few classmates who had features like mine - brown skin and thick, textured hair. They looked as bewildered as I felt.

It was 1970. I was eight years old. I knew that I had African ancestry, but I didn't know why someone would want me to "go back" to a place where I'd never been. I lived here, in the United States with mom and dad, just as their parents had, and their parents before them.

When I got home from school that afternoon my parents sat me down and told me that my classmate most likely heard that remark from her parents and simply repeated what they had said. This troubled me even more. We children had been around each other's parents at parent/teacher nights. My classmate's parents seemed like such nice people. I couldn't imagine why they would say something like that or feel that way about Black people.

Even though I was hurt by what my classmate said, I'd had enough religious training in my young years to understand the importance of not lashing out or trying to get even with her as children sometimes do. School went on as normal the next day with no mention of her remark by anyone.

It wasn't until years later that I realized that the incident wasn't isolated, that whole sectors of society were in agreement with the sentiments my classmate expressed or felt similarly about other groups of people based on race, gender, ethnicity, sexual identity, or other criteria.

I didn't know when I entered Kindergarten that my parents, having left the South because of the restrictions Jim Crow laws put on their lives, were not only protecting their shy child by choosing the small, private school, but had constructed an invisible wall around me with society's failings on the other side. They wanted me to have a carefree childhood like other children and only learn about the real world, with its biases and prejudices, when I was mature enough to understand. But because of my classmate's outburst, that life lesson got underway earlier than anticipated.

I never forgot the incident. I preserved it in my memory as a significant event and didn't tamp it down as just an insensitive remark. Not long after I'd graduated from college in the 1980s, my car was nearly run off the road as the driver of a car riding my bumper screamed racial slurs at me. When I was a television reporter in the 1990s in a Northeastern Pennsylvania community with very little ethnic diversity, I got anonymous messages left on my work voicemail from an angry viewer, shouting, "You're ugly. You're ugly. Why don't you go back where you came from!" Having once endured my classmate's "Go back to Africa" taunt helped to prepare me for those encounters and others to come, but didn't take away the pain. I shared details about what I had endured with a woman I befriended in an adult Sunday school class I was attending. She simply said, "Pray for them." I thought I hadn't heard her correctly and asked her to repeat herself. "They need help," she said. "The best thing you can do is to ask God to work on them."

I dismissed the idea at first. I felt that I was the one who needed to be prayed for. I needed God's protection from such hurtful people. But as I thought more about my friend's advice, I began to embrace it. Praying for them was important for my own maturation and spiritual growth. I realized that they were flawed individuals who needed compassion as God had shown me compassion through the years. I began to feel unburdened.

The words of Paul the Apostle underscore the soundness of my friend's advice. In a letter to the Colossians, he tells them what they must do to lead a truly Christian life. *Therefore as God's chosen people, holy and dearly loved, clothe yourselves with compassion, kindness, humility, gentleness and patience. (Colossians 3:12) (NIV).*

Ironically, the classmate who said that at the water fountain is one of the few people from elementary school I've seen since our 8th grade graduation and one of the few I've run into repeatedly on return trips to my hometown. Typically we end up at the same restaurant or the same store in the shopping mall. Each time, we reminisce about our school days and trade notes on what's happened in our classmates' lives and our own. Throughout these conversations, her outburst at the water fountain plays in my mind like a well-orchestrated movie score, evoking just enough tension to make me a little anxious. But I have never sensed any of the vitriol I felt from her that day. I've wondered if she remembers what she said that day. I doubt that she has any idea of the impact it had on me.

I suffered a monumental loss when my classmate had her outburst, a loss of innocence I could never regain. I also learned an important lesson. Skin color was all the reason a person needed to feel anger and hatred.

MESSIAH
BAPTIST CHURCH

Chapter 5
Dancing Between the Raindrops

I walk through a season of grief
Fields of heartache leave my feet blistered and raw
Optimism is shrouded by a pewter grey sky.
Hope muffled by fear and heartache
I am unprepared for this pilgrimage.
It used to be that I floated through seasons
Propelled by lush meadows
Richly colored blooms dazzling my eyes
I longed to take hold of those moments.
Freeze time, hit pause, frame them,
Knowing they would not last.

I have no choice now but to forge ahead
Through knotted weeds and thick crabgrass.
Wait for the sun showers to come
When new life blossoms
And the healing begins
Then I will dance between the raindrops
Savoring the joy between the storms
The laughter between the sorrow

My
Latest Hit

Chapter 6
Dad's Playlist

➤ Twistin' The Night Away 02:42
Sam Cooke

I watch you blow dust off the record player needle on the Hi-Fi stereo system and lower the arm onto the album as it spins around. My excitement builds as I hear a crackling sound coming from the speakers high up on the walls on opposite sides of the family room.

At 2 years old I am eye level with your knees. You reach your hand down to me and say, "May I have this dance? I tuck my tiny hand in your giant one and stand on your feet as you lead me, rocking back and forth to Sam Cooke's voice bouncing off the walls.

➤ The Christmas Song 0:3:31
Nat "King" Cole

It's Christmas Eve and I'm tucked in waiting for Santa and the reindeer to land on the roof. It's late at night, company has left, mom has gone to bed and you are in the basement drinking egg nog and playing The Christmas Song. I press my eyes shut and listen to the words, thinking I'll forget about how excited I am and go to sleep, the night will go fast and Santa will come down the chimney, leave my presents and drink eggnog with you.

➤ Auld Lang Syne 0:2:39
Guy Lombardo

It's New Year's Day and I crane my neck to look up at the living room ceiling. It's covered in balloons in different colors. At three and a half, I'm still little enough for you to pick me up. You hand me a thumb tack, tell me to be careful with it and put me on your shoulders. We go to each balloon. I aim just right and they go Pop! Pop! Pop! Last night I couldn't sleep for all the people and laughter and music from the party you and mom had. The last song I remember hearing was that song that was played at midnight.

➤ I'll Be Around 0:3:13
The Spinners

You like to whistle while you work, especially when a song comes on the urban contemporary radio station you have the stereo tuned to at the store. You whistle to "I'll Be Around" and customers bop to the beat. I help ring up sales, take inventory, dust, vacuum. Not a bad way for a teenager to pick up a few dollars to spend at the mall with her friends.

➤ Let's Stay Together 0:3:21
Al Green

You're at the wheel, mom's in the passenger seat and we kids, Sylvia and me, are in the back. It's another road trip "down South" to see the relatives for the annual homecoming at your church, St. Mary Baptist in Lowesville, Virginia on the first weekend in August. Throughout the ride from Connecticut to Virginia you and mom relive the indignities you faced growing up under Jim Crow laws. It's an instant history lesson for Sylvia and me. At moments, Mom's voice catches in her throat as she gets emotional. You turn on the 8-track tape player and Al Green starts his ballad, a needed break from the intensity of your reminiscences.

➤ What the World Needs Now is Love 03:06
Dionne Warwick

Nearly all of my friends wanted to be debutantes and even though I didn't know what a debutante was, I wanted to be one too. Mom had to explain it to me. It's all about us 17- and 18-year-olds making our debut into society. Mom told me that you didn't really want to be bothered with it, but because I wanted to be a "Deb," you agreed to it. We had weekly practice sessions with a choreographer to learn how to waltz. It's the night of the cotillion. We're halfway through our father/daughter dance and I'm worried that you'll forget to twirl me at the right moment. I take a deep breath. You do, in fact, forget to twirl me. But I cue you and all goes smoothly.

➤ What's Going On 0:3:53
Marvin Gaye

You spend Sunday afternoons in the basement of our home with the stereo on listening to "What's Going On." The song's lyrics touch on racism, drug abuse, poverty and the Vietnam War. This is your "alone time." No one interrupts you during these moments. I can't help but wonder if you're thinking about what's going on in your own life. The clothing store has been broken into many times, sometimes by people you'd hired to work there. The once bustling, relatively safe working-class neighborhood has become a haven for drug dealers and addicts. Your customer base is shrinking.

➤ Pachelbel's Canon in D0:6:12
Johann Pachelbel

You and I are standing at the French doors of the mansion that I've rented for my wedding. You're as spiffy as ever in your tuxedo. I'm in a full-length ivory gown, lovely for a "mature" bride of 52. As my pianist and cellist begin performing Pachelbel's Canon in D, the doors open. All the guests are standing, the accompaniment is so overwhelming that I feel momentarily dizzy. You escort me down the aisle and as you are giving me away, I realize that you have forgotten to kiss me on the cheek. I say repeatedly louder each time, "Kiss me on the cheek, Daddy," which you eventually do. The guests laugh. You and I laugh. My photographer captures the awkward moment, which becomes one of my favorite photos from my wedding.

➤ Unforgettable 02:32
Nat "King" Cole

Mom has passed away and you announce that you want to sing "Unforgettable" at her funeral. Because of your hearing loss, Parkinson's disease and dementia, I don't think you'll be able to do it. But each day leading up to the funeral, you read over the lyrics and practice. At the funeral, the pastor calls you to come forward. You struggle to stand up with your cane. Everyone there shouts, "take your time, take your time." You slowly get to the podium and sing the first verse. You are cheered. It is one of the most memorable moments of the funeral.

➤ Twistin' The Night Away 02:42
Sam Cooke

We've just returned to your room after having lunch in the dining room on the memory care floor of the assisted living center you've been staying at since Mom died last year. The aides have told me about your habits—going back to bed, putting your sheet over your face and taking a nap. After I fold up your walker, you do lie back down, but since I am visiting you stay awake and leave the flat sheet tucked neatly around the mattress. I surprise you by turning on my portable speaker and playing "Twistin' the Night Away." I extend my hand to you and ask, "May I have this dance?" as you asked me more than 55 years earlier. You shake your head and politely say, "I won't be able to do that today." I take your hands and swing them back and forth to the beat. Pretty soon you are swinging my hands back and forth and I don't have to make any effort. It's been years since I've seen you smile so broadly.

➤ I'll Fly Away 0:4:04
Alison Krauss

I'm at the front of the church gazing at you one last time before they close the casket. You look serene and I am glad. I worried about you every single day. I never knew when I would get a call from the aides that you'd fallen again. Sometimes I'd get a call from you telling me that you missed Mom. You could hardly speak you were crying so hard. Other times in your confusion you'd call me sounding out of breath and say that you were hungry, that you weren't being fed. I'd find out later that because of your dementia you didn't remember that you'd eaten.

You lived long enough to celebrate your 90th birthday surrounded by family and friends. You went downhill dramatically after the guests left. I'm pleased with the choices that Sylvia and I made for your "homegoing" suit. We chose to have you dressed in one of your favorites, a deep blue pinstripe suit with the silk pocket handkerchief, and bold striped tie. I felt jubilant when I found your Rotary Club lapel pin in your nightstand and had the mortuary place it on your lapel. You loved being a Rotarian and so did I. After you sponsored me, we'd attend Rotary meetings together.

I requested that one of the church choir soloists sing "I'll Fly Away" as she did for Mom's funeral. I couldn't help but wonder if you knew I was there as you flew away. I feel blessed that I got to spend your last days in the hospital room with you, got to kiss you on the forehead each night and tell you what a great dad you were and that I loved you, that I got to listen to the spaces between each of your breaths until you had no more.

➤ Taps 0:3:03
The U.S. Army

At the cemetery an Army rifle squad fired a three-volley salute and a bugler played Taps. As the shells from the salute were placed in my palm, I thought of your service stateside during the Korean War era before you married Mom. Those two years had a profound effect on how you helped Mom raise me, a blend of order and discipline, sprinkled with humor and fun. I clasped those shells in my hand and watched as the U.S. flag was meticulously folded and tucked. Then placed on my lap. I am honored by your service to our country, honored to be your daughter.

Sometimes when I'm turning the dial on my car radio or tune into the music piped in at the supermarket or a coffee shop, I'll hear one of the songs on your playlist. I'll take a breath and steel myself so that I won't become weepy in public. I'll think about the memories linked to the song. Usually, I'll smile.

This is what a

Chapter 7
Checkerboard Dance Floor

You skipped down the basement stairs, two at a time
Like a performer in the grand finale of a musical
Stopping only when you'd landed in the family room
On the checkerboard tile floor that you'd installed
Where we watched movies and played Atari tennis, flipping the knob with just the right wrist action
Back and forth
Back and forth
Where you and mom invited friends from your factory jobs
Played 45s on the Hi-Fi - Aretha, Marvin, Wilson, Gladys
Shimmying down the Soul Train line before there was a Soul Train
Arms flapping the funky chicken, hips shifting and swaying the pony
Where you and mom operated your real estate firm

We listened from afar when you played your cerebral jazz albums on Sunday afternoons after
church, hard bop rollicking saxophone riffs that only appealed
to you.

Lisa Braxton

Pristine wood-paneled walls gradually populated with markers of your success.
Gold-plated plaques and framed "grip and grin" photos
NAACP President!
Black-owned business owner!
City Alderman!
Sponsor of causes in the community!
Now the plaques are packed away.
Warped jazz albums in a haphazard pile, a layer of dust obscuring the covers like scratches on a worn 45 rendering the sound muffled
The real estate firm folded long ago
High-Fi no longer spinning tunes
Friends passed on or moved back Down South
A distant memory, the skip down the stairs.

Now you wrestle with them
Shakily and slowly taking them one at a time
Gripping your cane with one hand and pulling yourself along on the railing, like a grade school choir soloist searching for the right key.
Running up and down the scales, flailing until the right key presents itself.
Sometimes the stairs win and you tumble in your frailty.
Legs buckling beneath you.
I want to pick you up, take you back to the grand finale of the musical
Back to the freshly polished checkerboard dance floor.

Chapter 8
Missing Person

NIGHTLY NEWSCAST SCRIPT

VIDEO	AUDIO
NIGHTLY NEWS OPENER	(MUSIC INTRO)
2-SHOT OF ANCHORS	
	ANCHOR 1: WE BEGIN OUR BROADCAST TONIGHT WITH THE CASE OF A MISSING PERSON.
	ANCHOR 2: LOCAL POLICE CONTINUE THEIR SEARCH FOR RETIRED BUSINESS OWNER AND FORMER ALDERMAN JULIAN BRAXTON.

ANCHOR 1: IN HIS 80s ,
BRAXTON WAS REPORTED
MISSING FROM HIS HOME
THIS AFTERNOON.

(MUSIC FADE TO BED...)

HEADSHOT OF BRAXTON

ANCHOR 2:
AS THE HOURS
GO BY WITH NO WORD
ON HIS WHEREABOUTS, THE FAMILY
IS GROWING INCREASINGLY
CONCERNED.

2 SHOT ANCHOR 1 AND REPORTER LIVE

ANCHOR 1:
WE NOW GO LIVE
TO REPORTER S.J. LEE
WHO IS IN FRONT OF
THE POLICE DEPARTMENT
WITH THE LATEST. S.J.?

SINGLE SHOT LIVE WITH REPORTER

S.J. LEE.: I CHECKED WITH
POLICE MOMENTS AGO
AND THEY TOLD ME THAT
TWO POLICE OFFICERS
HAVE BEEN

VIDEO OF SQUAD CAR LEAVING
HEADQUARTERS PARKING LOT/
BRIDGEPORT LOCATIONS

ASSIGNED TO THE CASE.
THEIR SQUAD CAR HAS BEEN
CIRCLING THE CITY
IN SEARCH OF BRAXTON.
IN ADDITION, I'M TOLD
HIS NEPHEW HAS BEEN DRIVING

PHOTOS OF BRAXTON

AROUND FOR HOURS IN
HIS OWN SEARCH.
BRAXTON IS DESCRIBED
AS 5 FEET 10 INCHES TALL,
WEIGHS ABOUT
1-HUNDRED FIFTY POUNDS
AND HAS BROWN HAIR,
BROWN EYES AND WEARS GLASSES.

NEWSPAPER CLIPPINGS AND
FILE PHOTOS OF FRONT OF BRAXTON'S

YOU MAY RECALL THAT
BRAXTON IS AN ICON
IN THE COMMUNITY,
AN ACTIVIST WHO SERVED
ON CITY COUNCIL
AND WAS PRESIDENT OF THE
GREATER BRIDGEPORT BRANCH
OF THE NAACP,
IN ADDITION TO OWNING
AND OPERATING
A MEN'S CLOTHING STORE.
IN RECENT MONTHS,
BRAXTON HAS BEEN KNOWN
TO LEAVE HIS HOME
WITHOUT TELLING ANYONE,
WALKING ON HIS CANE.
THE FAMILY SAYS THAT
HE HAS PARKINSON'S DISEASE,
WHICH MAKES WALKING DIFFICULT.
HE LIKES TO FREQUENT
THE CONVENIENCE STORES
IN HIS NEIGHBORHOOD AND
OTHER PARTS OF TOWN,
BUT SO FAR HE HASN'T
BEEN SEEN IN THOSE LOCATIONS.
WITH NIGHTFALL,
FAMILY AND POLICE ARE

SINGLE SHOT LIVE WITH REPORTER

CONCERNED THAT MOTORISTS
MAY NOT SEE HIM AS HE CROSSES STREETS
ADD TO THAT, THE TEMPERATURE IS
FORECAST TO DIP INTO THE 30s TONIGHT,
WHICH RAISES ADDITIONAL CONCERNS
ABOUT BRAXTON.
REPORTING LIVE FROM
BRIDGEPORT POLICE HEADQUARTERS,
I'M S.J. LEE

2-SHOT ANCHOR 1 AND REPORTER

THANK YOU S.J. LEE
FOR THAT REPORT.
WE'LL KEEP YOU ON
THE SCENE IN CASE
THERE ARE ANY UPDATES
BEFORE THE END
OF OUR BROADCAST.

SINGLE SHOT OF ANCHOR 1

WE ARE ASKING THE
PUBLIC TO CONTACT THE
BRIDGEPORT POLICE DEPARTMENT
AT THE NUMBER ON
THE BOTTOM OF
YOUR SCREEN IF YOU HAVE ANY
INFORMATION ABOUT THE
WHEREABOUTS OF JULIAN BRAXTON

Chapter 9
Missing Person Folo

NIGHTLY NEWSCAST SCRIPT

VIDEO	AUDIO
BREAKING NEWS GRAPHIC 2-SHOT OF ANCHORS	
	ANCHOR 1: WE HAVE BREAKING NEWS AT THIS HOUR.
	ANCHOR 2: LAST NIGHT, WE TOLD YOU ABOUT THE SEARCH FOR RETIRED BUSINESS OWNER AND FORMER ALDERMAN JULIAN BRAXTON.

ANCHOR 1:
IN HIS 80s, BRAXTON WAS
REPORTED MISSING
FROM HIS HOME
YESTERDAY AFTERNOON.

HEADSHOT OF BRAXTON

ANCHOR 2:
TONIGHT, BRAXTON
IS BACK HOME SAFE
WITH HIS FAMILY.

2-SHOT ANCHOR 1 AND REPORTER LIVE

ANCHOR 1:
WE NOW GO LIVE
TO REPORTER S.J. WHO IS IN FRONT
OF THE BRAXTON HOME
WITH LATE, BREAKING DETAILS, S.J.?

SINGLE SHOT LIVE WITH REPORTER

REPORTER S.J.:
THIS IS TRULY A GOOD NEWS STORY.
MOMENTS AGO,
I SPOKE WITH FAMILY MEMBERS
WHO SAY THEY ARE RELIEVED TO HAVE
JULIAN BRAXTON HOME AND THEY HAVE
A KIND CITIZEN TO THANK FOR THAT.
I WAS ABLE TO TRACK DOWN

THE MAN WHO BROUGHT
BRAXTON HOME SAFELY.
HE SAID HE FOUND THE ELDERLY MAN
ABOUT A MILE FROM HERE,
TRYING TO CROSS THE
ENTRANCE RAMP OF THE HIGHWAY.
HE WANTS TO REMAIN ANONYMOUS SO WE'VE BLURRED HIS FACE.
HERE'S WHAT ELSE HE HAD TO SAY.

SOT BRIDGEPORT RESIDENT

I DON'T WANT ANY MEDALS.
I DON'T WANT ANY CREDIT FOR THIS.
I DID WHAT ANYBODY ELSE WOULD DO.
I SEEN HIM ON THE SIDEWALK,
STEPPING ONTO THE RAMP
ON HIS CANE. AND I SAID TO MYSELF,
'HE COULD GET HISSELF KILLED!'
I PULLED MY CAR OVER AND SAID,
"WHERE YOU LIVE? I'LL TAKE YOU HOME.
HE SAID 'NO NO NO'
I CAN'T GET IN YOUR CAR.'
SO I WALK HIM ALL THE WAY
BACK TO HIS HOUSE."

SINGLE SHOT LIVE WITH REPORTER

AND THE DISTANCE BETWEEN
THE ENTRANCE RAMP
AND THE BRAXTON HOUSE
IS ABOUT TWO MILES.
IF NOT FOR THAT RESIDENT,
WE MIGHT HAVE A VERY
DIFFERENT STORY
TO REPORT TO YOU TONIGHT.

2-SHOT WITH ANCHORS AND REPORTER

ANCHOR 1:
S.J., DO WE HAVE ANY IDEA
WHY BRAXTON WAS ON THAT RAMP
OR WHERE HE WAS GOING?

REPORTER S.J.:
HIS FAMILY DOESN'T KNOW.
THEY DID SAY THAT HE'S BEEN KNOWN
TO DO THIS SOMETIMES, GET RESTLESS AND WALK
OUT OF THE HOUSE WITHOUT
TELLING ANYONE. HIS DAUGHTER, LISA, DID SAY THAT
HE HAS PARKINSON'S DISEASE
AND THE FAMILY IS LOOKING INTO
GETTING SOME "CARE" FOR HIM.
THEY WOULDN'T GET SPECIFIC ON WHAT THAT CARE
WOULD BE.

2-SHOT ANCHOR 1 AND REPORTER

ANCHOR 1:
THANK YOU S.J.
FOR THAT REPORT
AND THAT GOOD NEWS.

2-SHOT OF ANCHORS

BRAXTON'S CONDITION
HIGHLIGHTS THE CHALLENGES
FAMILY MEMBERS FACE
WHEN CARING FOR AN
ELDERLY LOVED ONE
WHO HAS PARKINSON'S DISEASE.

PARKINSON'S GRAPHIC

TOMORROW NIGHT
WE BEGIN A 3-PART SERIES
CALLED "PARKINSON'S DISEASE:
THE LONG JOURNEY."
WE HOPE YOU'LL TUNE IN.

THE TALKING DRUM

Chapter 10
My Biggest Champion

"I sold another book."

Mom had persuaded another person to buy my novel. She was my champion. But her voice was getting weaker. When doctors said there was nothing more they could do, I moved back home. As the cancer metastasized, she wasn't very lucid, but one day pointed at her bookshelf.

"I left you something."

Earlier she'd had me tuck a few dollars next to her copy of my book.

"Next to *The Talking Drum*?" I asked. She put on a big smile,

"Yes! *The Talking Drum*!" That moment is one of my greatest treasures. Mom died days later.

Chapter 11
Our Messes

"This place is a mess," my father said in a stern voice, surprising me as he looked around the room. "Are you going to clean it?"

Not sure how to respond, I simply said, "Yes."

He nodded, then strode out of my childhood bedroom on his cane, forgetting that he was elderly, that I had grown up and moved out decades earlier, that he was the one who made the mess.

You can't go back to the past. But my father's dementia briefly let me relive a moment from the 1960s, when I was his little girl.

Chapter 12
The Bonds of Battle

On an early Sunday morning in June, I woke and unplugged my phone from its charger. I had three missed calls from my sister and a voicemail message from her. My heart pounded as I listened to Sylvia's message, punctuated with dead air as she paused to cry. My mother had been rushed to the hospital. Her white cell count was alarming. She had a severe infection. The growth in her colon had enlarged dramatically. She might not live another 24 hours if doctors didn't intervene. But if doctors tried to remove the growth, she might not be strong enough to survive surgery. Doctors wanted the family to come together to make a decision immediately.

On autopilot, I texted my parents' pastor to alert him to what was going on and asked for prayer. Pastor Logan responded immediately. He was preparing to give that morning's sermon, but said he would send the deacons to the hospital to pray at my mother's bedside. He would go to see her after service.

I showered, dressed, and tossed clothes and toiletries into a suitcase and was on the road within three hours. The trip from Weymouth, Massachusetts to Bridgeport, Connecticut is two and a half to three hours. My sister and brother-in-law, in Rockville, Maryland, packed up the kids and the dogs and got on the road for their six-hour drive, not long after I pulled onto the highway.

At 57, I had never experienced this degree of stress before. Only a few weeks earlier I had undergone a painful MRI biopsy, the final tests confirming what the doctors had suspected—that I had breast cancer. Chemotherapy would not be an appropriate treatment for my type of cancer, they said. Radiation was a possibility. I opted for a lumpectomy, which was scheduled for later.

An hour into my 70-mile-per-hour drive down Interstate 95 toward Connecticut, my aunt, who was with my mother at the hospital, texted me:

Would you like to speak with your mother?

I texted back while gripping the steering wheel with one hand:

Yes.

I could only think that this would be the last conversation I had with my mother. She might be gone before I could get to the medical center. When the call came in on the car's Wi-Fi system, she could barely talk.

"I'm on my way, Mommy," I shouted at the car speaker. "Hang on! I just passed through Providence. I'll be there soon. I love you."

Somehow, she managed to screech a word: "Okay."

Mom was 82. It was unreasonable for me to expect my time with her to be unlimited. Since childhood I'd watched classmates and friends suffer the loss of a parent. With each death I imagined Mom, Dad, Sylvia and me on a battlefield, ducking into a foxhole as ammo whizzed over our heads, missing us, but taking out other families. Maybe it was finally my family's turn to take a bullet.

At the hospital, under the bright fluorescent lights I race-walked down the corridor to Mom's room, a combination of antiseptic and food smells filling my nostrils. Peeking around the oversized private-room door I caught sight of my aunt calmly sitting in a chair facing the hospital bed. My mother must still be alive. I felt lighter, the sound of my heartbeat pounding in my ears dissipated. I braced myself and absorbed the scene. Mom was hooked up to machines, her eyes shut, her skin ashen, her hands trembling. I grasped them, they were ice cold.

Dabbing at the corners of her eyes with a tissue, my aunt explained that the emergency response people contacted her. Mom had passed out at home in the hallway by the bathroom. Dad had pushed the medic alert button. A neighbor stayed with them until the ambulance took mom away.

"Mommy, how are you feeling?" I asked.

She could only mutter half sentences.

"Cold," she eventually said.

I mashed the button to the nurse's station. A nurse came in and wrapped her in another blanket. Minutes later, Mom's temperature was checked. It had jumped to 102. A nurse wheeled in a tray stacked with bags of ice, tucked some around Mom and covered her with the rest.

Later, the doctor arrived, a tall woman with a Caribbean accent and a warm brown skin similar to mine. I tried to push away the queasiness in my stomach as she said the tumor appeared to be cancerous and repeated the gist of what the overnight doctor had said to my sister. *Do nothing and your mother will pass away within days. Operate and she may not survive.*

"What would *you* do?" I asked her. "What would you do if this was your mother or sister?" The doctor paused for a long moment. "It all depends on your mother. She may feel that she's lived her life and wants to go peacefully. Or she may want to fight." I got the doctor's permission to record her prognosis and insight and texted it to my sister. Her family now had the George Washington Bridge in sight, which was about an hour and a half away.

Months earlier mom began experiencing pain in her abdominal area. Her doctor ordered a colonoscopy, concluded that she had diverticulitis, an inflammation of the bowels, and that there was a blockage causing her bleeding. After a follow-up colonoscopy, which was inconclusive, he recommended that she see a specialist. The specialist recommended that she have surgery. It took weeks to get clearance from her primary care doctor who put her through a series of tests to make sure that as an 82-year-old woman she was strong enough for the surgery. Mom told me that she would be relieved to have the surgery, she was in so much pain and the blood loss made her uncomfortable going out in public.

Finally, clearance in hand, she went back to the surgeon. He scheduled the procedure to remove the growth for a month later. However, before the procedure could be done, she passed out at home in the hallway outside of the bathroom and was rushed to the medical center.

"We've taken another look at your mother's X-rays," the doctor announced later that night with the entire family now gathered at my mother's bedside. "We want to take a step back. The X-ray technician sees that your mother has been living with this for some time. And the antibiotics seem to be working. Her white cell count has gone down a bit. It is possible to stabilize her and not even consider surgery at the moment. Let's monitor her and see if the antibiotics continue to work."

We all breathed sighs of relief. Mom's color was returning to normal and she was able to have full-length conversations with us, having no idea how sick she was. As the days passed, Mom continued to get better. Amid tearful goodbyes I returned to Massachusetts. My aunt vowed to stay at Mom's side for the duration of her recovery. A steady stream of friends and church leaders had assured us that they would continue to surround Mom with love and prayers.

I returned to work and felt comfortable enough with Mom's progress to get on a plane for an already-planned business trip to San Antonio. I resumed a measure of normalcy with my mother's health crisis tucked in the back of my mind and my scheduled cancer surgery for the following week bubbling up to the surface of my consciousness.

However, the day after I landed in Texas, I got an urgent text from my aunt asking me to listen to the recording she had just sent me from the doctor. My aunt wanted my sister and me to weigh in before a decision was made. I stepped into a hallway away from the educational session I was attending. My stomach roiled as I listened to the recording. My mother's white cell count was rising again. The blockage in the infected area was beginning to close. It was recommended that surgery be done as soon as possible. Or my mother could be discharged, go home, and make an appointment to see her original surgeon, who didn't have privileges at the medical center, but at a hospital across town.

"I can get that tumor out," I heard the doctor, who I'd met days earlier, say in a strong, confident voice on the recording.

My sister, aunt, and I were in agreement to proceed with the operation. The doctor scheduled surgery for early the next morning —my birthday. My sister and family were back in Maryland and packed for a return trip to Bridgeport. I was in agony. If I could have predicted that surgery would be in Mom's future so soon, I wouldn't have gone on the business trip. With the flight connections required to get into and out of San Antonio, I knew I couldn't get back to Bridgeport in time.

I called my mother, trying to reassure her moments before they wheeled her into the operating room. She started to cry. "I don't want you and Sylvia to be sad if I don't make it." I assured her that she would come through surgery, but silently wondered if she would.

I prayed that she would be all right. Halfway through the procedure my sister texted me that the surgery was going smoothly. Later, I got another text from her stating that my mother was in recovery. The surgeon had removed the growth and made clean margins around the area. This was by far the best birthday gift I had ever received!

The pathology report confirmed that the growth was indeed cancerous and in an advanced stage. In the abstract I'd always assumed I would crumble if my mother faced a life-threatening illness, fall into a heap of tears and be useless. But, in actuality, I was determined to be strong for Mom as she recovered and would undergo further treatment. I was surprised at my reaction.

As I was wheeled into my own surgery the following week, I vowed to build her up as she had done for me when I told her about my diagnosis.

"You're going to be fine," she had said. "They caught it early. You're going to be just fine. I know it."

I would remind her that she wasn't alone in her illness, that we would draw strength from each other as we fought cancer together.

Chapter 13
Pajama Party for Two

My mother attended her first pajama party when she was 83 years old. And that was because I decided to host it for her. As her health began to fail her world became very small. Appointments with the physical therapist who guided her on short walks through the house had been canceled. The nurse's aide who'd gotten her into the shower and then later could only give her sponge baths at her bedside had been told not to come back. The prepared dinners from Meals on Wheels were stacked high in the refrigerator and were barely touched.

I packed a couple of suitcases, kissed my husband good-bye and headed out the door after Mom's doctor let us know that there was nothing more to be done to treat the ovarian cancer. The cancer had metastasized and was spreading rapidly.

"Make new memories. Enjoy this time," her doctor had said.

I kept that thought in mind during the road trip back home.

One morning, I raised Mom's bed to a sitting position and we watched one of her favorite talk shows, The View. She'd always enjoyed the gossip, entertainment news, political banter and clashing and barbs among the co-hosts.

The women were talking excitedly about the vice-presidential debate to be broadcast nationwide that night. It was October 7,

2020. Vice President Mike Pence and Senator Kamala Harris would have their one and only debate before the presidential election on November 3rd.

Excitement had been building in our family for weeks, ever since Harris had been announced as Joe Biden's running mate. Harris was our sorority sister. Harris, Mom and I were members of Alpha Kappa Alpha Sorority, Inc., which has a largely African American membership across the United States and other countries numbering in the hundreds of thousands, undergraduate and graduate chapter members, women committed to service and sisterhood.

As the ladies on The View speculated on the Pence-Harris matchup and the debate's outcome, I said to Mom, "Let's have a pajama party."

She gave me a weak smile. "How are we going to do that?"

Obviously, this would not be a typical pajama party, the kind I got invited to when I was a little girl with lots of giggling, pillow fights, and plugging in the E-Z Bake Oven at 2 in the morning to make a pancake-size German chocolate cake. It would be an opportunity for Mom and me to have mother/daughter time, knowing that our time together would soon come to an end.

"We'll have it right here. I'll take care of everything."

"Okay," she said. Her eyelids fluttered shut as she dozed for a nap.

Preparation would be simple. No food would need to be cooked; no popcorn popped, or bags of chips opened. Mom ate little and took in as much liquid as she needed to swallow her pain medication and anti-nausea pills, but not much more. Obviously, no travel was required. Party central would be Mom's hospital bed brought in for her hospice care weeks earlier. Dad would stay on the upper floor in my old childhood bedroom. He was happy to do so. He was four years older than Mom and had lost most of his hearing. We'd have the volume on the TV much too low for him. There was no need to invite additional partiers. What was that old saying about "two's company"?

That evening, about an hour before the debate, I changed into my pajamas and helped mom get into hers. A sorority sister had given her the pajamas after Mom's return from one of her several hospital stays, pink and green, our sorority colors, with Mom's name emblazoned across the back like on an athlete's uniform.

I carefully eased the top over her head and the cute afro she now had after her hair grew back once her chemo treatment had ended. As I awkwardly threaded her weak arms through the sleeves, I accidentally brushed my knuckles across her nose.

"Oh! You broke my nose! You broke my nose!" she cried out. Mom still had her sense of humor. I'd barely grazed the tip of her nose. I decided to go along with the joke.

"Why did you break my nose?" she continued.

"I'll tell you what," I said. "Since I broke your nose, you can break mine. Then we'll be even."

"I could never do that," she said, becoming serious.

"Yes, you can," I said.

I took her hand and balled it up into a fist and brushed it against my nose. "My nose is broken now too and it hurts really bad. Oh, Mommy, I can't believe you broke my nose."

Mom laughed. "You're so silly."

I fluffed Mom's pillow and pressed a button on the bed's remote control so that she could sit up comfortably. I pulled out my cell phone and had us take selfies. Then on impulse I said, "Strike a pose, Mommy, like you're a model!"

To my surprise, she obliged, flinging her arms this way and that, raising her chin, tilting her head as I coaxed her along for different poses. Every so often she'd say, "Is this what you want? Am I doing it right?"

Mom had always been very reserved. She grew up in the 1940s and '50s in a multigenerational household in which children were taught to be seen and not heard. Scolding and punishment didn't just come from her mother, but anyone else in the house —aunts, uncles, grandparents. Mom said she would often retreat to her room and read a book to stay out of the way and avoid anyone's wrath. She mentioned this often as I was growing up, resentment laced in her words. This helped me to understand why she often seemed so restrained.

I took one picture after another. Decades earlier I don't know if I could have convinced her to be that spontaneously playful. But I feel she knew the importance of the moment and thought about how one day I wouldn't have her anymore.

Mom's world had become small, spatially small, but I found a way for us to have a big party for two that would have us smiling throughout the evening. And making new memories.

Chapter 14
Press Release

For Immediate Release (May 12, 2017)

Former Clothing Store Demolished to Make Way for Redevelopment

(Bridgeport, CT) – As neighborhood residents watched, demolition got underway at a building that once housed one of the longest running businesses in the East End of the city. Mayor Joe Ganim, at the controls of a steam shovel, tore down Braxton's Men's Shop.

Braxton's was a neighborhood landmark for close to 50 years, supplying formal wear for graduations, proms and cotillions. Julian Braxton, a former member of the Bridgeport City Council and former president of the Greater Bridgeport Branch of the NAACP, did not attend the demolition.

Other buildings on the block owned by Braxton and his wife, Elizabeth, are being torn down.

"Braxton's was a family business," said his daughter Lisa. "My parents co-owned it. My mother worked here alongside my father. My sister and I practically grew up here. When we were kids, Dad had us taking inventory, processing payments to vendors, going on buying trips with him to wholesalers in Manhattan."

"Dad has a big heart," she continued. "He made a point of hiring high schoolers to work at the store and sponsored the East End Little League for many years, paying for their uniforms and equipment. He would speak at their end of the year banquet. Those kids loved it."

Last year city officials abandoned plans to seize the building by eminent domain after community activists demanded that the Braxton's be compensated for the properties or that they have some say in the plans before eminent domain was authorized.

City council voted to compensate the Braxton's.

The redevelopment proposal calls for building between 30 and 60 apartments, a small grocery store providing ethnic food and a new library.

Community leaders at the demolition said they are cautiously optimistic that the new development will help revitalize that section of the city, which had become blighted and crime-ridden.

Chapter 15
The Driver

The doorbell rang on a crisp October morning, the day after Mom's funeral. My sister, Sylvia, and I were not surprised. During Mom's home hospice, the bell rang throughout the day. Relatives, friends, Mom's club sisters and church deacons would drop by unexpectedly, sometimes with cakes or casseroles. Sometimes with tears in their eyes.

So when the bell rang the morning after the funeral, Sylvia and I didn't bother to peek through the curtain to see who was there. We were lounging on Mom and Dad's bed, surrounded by items no longer needed, packages of bed pads, oxygen tanks, a bedside commode chair, a remote-control hospital bed. All stark reminders that Mom was gone.

"I'll go see who it is," I volunteered. Sylvia, her face pressed into a pillow, gave a muffled, "Okay."

I felt numb when I opened the door, as if I was a spectator floating somewhere in the ceiling looking down at myself. I was emotionally spent. The worst had already happened. My mother was dead. A police officer standing on the porch was no big deal.

"Ma'am, we got a call about a stolen car."

The only other time I could recall the police coming to my parents' house was years earlier when I'd walked in alone one day, couldn't remember the alarm system code and frantically mashed different button combinations while the ear-splitting alarm wailed. The alarm company summoned the police. I'd assured the officer that I was safe.

"Sir, no car's been stolen." I gestured toward the candy apple red Toyota SUV parked in the driveway. "The car's right there."

The officer looked in the direction of the driveway and then back at me. "So, what's going on?"

It didn't take me long to figure out who called the police. The night before, hours after we'd returned home from Mom's funeral, our 88-year-old father made a demand.

"I want to drive your mother's car," he said in a stern voice. "I need the keys."

Sylvia and I exchanged a panicked look. I tried to think of a response that wouldn't get him further agitated. Dad had always been mild-mannered and easy-going with us. We were his princesses. He spoiled us well into adulthood. It was painful watching his temperament gradually change when he reached his late 70s. Responding to one of his requests with *No, I can't*, or *I don't think so* could result in an explosive outburst. He'd been diagnosed with Parkinson's disease, which likely explained his irritability and cognitive impairment.

Dad was losing his ability to view matters logically or express shades of meaning. The concepts of danger and safety had become lost to him. His driving made Sylvia and me nervous.

Most of the decisions and negotiations that had to be made behind the wheel were beyond him now. Stop signs and traffic signals became mere suggestions that he chose to ignore.

He'd had four accidents in his car the year before Mom died. The police suspended his license and gave him a court date. He refused to go to court and kept driving.

He drove to city hall once for an appointment, couldn't find a parking space and drove the car up onto a sidewalk and left it there. It turns out the meeting was nonexistent. He was issued a ticket. He never paid it.

Eventually he totaled his car. Sylvia and I were relieved, but not for long. He started driving Mom's car, a Toyota SUV, against both her wishes and our gentle suggestions that he stop.

Fearful for pedestrians and motorists I called the police, pleading with them to make my father stop driving. They said they couldn't. They'd have to witness him driving erratically in order to impound the SUV.

Despite his deteriorating mental state, he was clever enough to keep the car keys in his pants pocket whenever he returned home. Sylvia and I were on high alert, waiting for him to slip up and leave the keys where we could find them. Eventually he did. Sylvia found the keys on the kitchen table one afternoon inside of his baseball cap. She gleefully snatched them up and hid them in Mom and Dad's bedroom closet in a nondescript gift box wedged in Mom's shoe organizer.

"Daddy, we don't know where the keys are," I lied, using a soft, child-like daughter tone. I glanced at Sylvia for reinforcement.

"Anyway, Daddy, it's dark outside," she chimed in.

"Yeah, Daddy," I added. "Everything's shut down. There's no place to go."

Dad got that faraway look in his eyes he'd had in recent years, as if he was trying to grasp a thought just beyond his reach. "Everything's shut down?" he finally asked.

"Yes, Daddy," we said in unison.

He seemed to calm down. Haltingly he pivoted on his cane and slowly walked away.

"I've been driving for 65 years and I'm not stopping now!"

For years that was Dad's refrain whenever Sylvia or I broached the topic of him getting an Uber or Lyft account or the idea that he and Mom take the train to make the 400-mile trip to visit Sylvia and her family in Maryland. I lived closer, in the Boston area, only a two and a half hour drive away from Mom and Dad in Connecticut. I made a point to visit often enough that Dad had no reason to think about planning a car trip north.

Based on stories he'd tell Sylvia and me when we were kids, he'd actually been driving longer than he calculated. Dad grew up in a farming community in Virginia. He said he learned to drive a tractor when he was 10. "If you can drive a tractor, you can drive a car," he'd told us.

Having a car was central to Mom and Dad's courtship. They grew up in the 1940s and '50s in the same region of Virginia but dozens of miles apart. Neither had a phone in their household, but Dad had a car. He'd drive to my mother's grandmother's house and ask for Mom. If she wasn't home, he'd drive off and swing back around later.

They had a traditional 1950s marriage. Dad had the last word on all major decisions. Whenever Mom and Dad were in the car at the same time, Dad drove, Mom rode shotgun, Sylvia and me in the back. On Sundays after church, Dad would steer the car to the Fairfield County suburbs, cruise through the neighborhoods of the wealthy with their manicured lawns, power washed circular driveways and low stone walls to let us see how we could live if we did well in school, went to college and had successful careers.

He was behind the wheel for longer drives each August from Connecticut to Virginia for homecoming with his siblings and other family at the small Baptist church in the village where he grew up.

Decades later it was heartbreaking to think about how safe I had felt with Dad driving and how terrifying the thought of it had become in later years.

When I told the officer that Mom's funeral was the day before and described Dad's demand for the keys, he radioed into headquarters that the call about a stolen car was actually a domestic situation.

"I'm sorry you came all the way out here for nothing," I said.

"We have to," he said. "When we get a call, we have to come out."

Not long after the officer left, Dad nudged the bedroom door open with his cane and found Sylvia and me there. I began wringing my hands to calm myself.

"I called the cops," he sounded as stern as he did the night before. "Did they get here yet?"

Sylvia and I exchanged a look. “The car’s in the driveway, Daddy,” I said. “No one took it.”

“If the keys are missing, we need to report it,” he said, “let the cops know. Someone could steal the car.”

I wasn’t sure of Dad’s motivation for wanting to drive the SUV. Was it because he missed Mom? Did he want to spend time in one of the possessions that had brought her the most joy in her later years? Did he want to assert his legal right to drive the car, or was it something else?

Perhaps, after decades of independence, of feeling in control of nearly every aspect of his life, of always being the driver in the family literally and otherwise, and then slowly losing that independence, losing his mental and physical abilities, he felt the need to assert himself.

I couldn’t blame him.

For months his sister-in-law, Mom’s caretaker, had let herself into the house every day to look after her and help manage the household in ways he no longer could. His daughters were trying to “mother” him, dissuading him from partaking in activities he had enjoyed all of his adult life. He may have perceived these actions as patronizing and insulting. He may have felt his role as the patriarch was being usurped.

By calling the police, Dad made a statement. That he was still relevant, that he was still here, that he was still the driver.

4
5
6
7
8
9
10
11
12
13
14
15
16
17
18
19

Chapter 16
Parenting the Parents

"Dad, there's something we need to talk about," I said. Sylvia and I spent hours trying to get him to sit down at the kitchen table for a conversation.

(8 down: The act of keeping away from or not doing something)

I took a deep breath once he sat down to steady myself for what I wanted to say next. "You're 82. We think it's time for you to retire."

(10 across: The act of interceding with the intent of modifying the outcome)

Dad looked from Sylvia to me, then into the distance just above our heads with a gleam in his eye. "I have a plan. There's a space on East Main Street where I can open another store." I wondered if he'd heard what I said, so I repeated myself and added, "Dad, you need to relax, to enjoy the rest of your life."

(2 down: Two words, the time of life after retirement)

It's a good space, a good location," he continued. "I can have all the merchandise sent over there. I can set up in a matter of days, get some flyers printed." I began to realize that Dad's identity was consumed by the business. Without it, he seemed lost.

(12 across: An idea or thought that continually preoccupies or intrudes on a person's mind)

Mom and Dad received a check for some property they had owned since the 1970s. After the sale, Dad's behavior became bizarre. I told a doctor friend about some incidents, and she said "that sounds like dementia." I thought that was ridiculous. Sylvia did too. He lost his temper every so often, which was a new behavior for him. He'd always been mild mannered. He was still Dad.

(4 down: A sentimental longing or wistful affection for the past, typically for a period or place with happy personal associations)

When I suggested the possibility of dementia to my mother, she admonished me. "I'm going to tell your father you said that!"

(13 across: To draw someone's attention away from something)

Dad didn't seem to have memory issues, could drive just fine, still had a sense of humor and spoke in a coherent fashion. He and Mom played cards on the weekend and he often won. I told myself he was simply going through a crisis because the store was shut down.

(5 down: The act of declaring something to be untrue)

"Dad, you don't have your business license anymore," Sylvia said. "If you opened another store, that would be illegal." He was still not making eye contact with us. "The building has two entrances," he said. "One will be the entrance to Braxton's. Customers will know they're there because I'm going to do it up nice. Have plush carpeting installed."

(14 across: Behaving in a mechanical or unemotional manner)

Mom walked into the kitchen to get a glass of water. "See what I mean, girls?" she said. "All he thinks about is that store. I wanted us to enjoy ourselves, take it easy. Travel. But he won't do that. Talk to him all you want, but it's not going to make a difference."

(3 down: Unwilling to change or compromise)

"Don't you want to enjoy your grandchildren, Dad?" I asked. "You and Mom could take the train to Maryland, relax, spend time with them." In recent years, Dad continued to insist on driving, even though his reaction to road situations had slowed dramatically and he guzzled high-caffeine drinks to stay awake. "I'm not going without my car," he said, tension in his voice.

(6 across: Having or showing dogged determination not to change one's attitude or position on something, especially in spite of good arguments or reasons to do so)

At some point, if they live long enough, we have to parent our parents, to find a way to parent them without them realizing what we're doing, especially if they're too proud to go along with it. At the kitchen table, I felt that I was failing at my efforts to parent my father, to protect him from himself.

(1 down: The feeling of being upset or annoyed, especially because of an inability to change or achieve something)

We knew that Dad was becoming agitated. If we continued with our prodding, he would get angry, Sylvia and I would get upset and nothing would be accomplished.

(11 down: Having feelings that are easily excited and openly displayed)

We pivoted to a topic that was non confrontational. Later, Sylvia told me she'd write a letter outlining all the reasons why he should not open another store. I said that I would call him in a few weeks reiterating the same.

(7 across: A list of steps that shows how to achieve an objective, goal or purpose)

We were determined to get him to see reality, to convince him and Mom to move into a new phase of their lives, which was best for them.

(5 down: A view or judgment formed about something, not necessarily based on fact or knowledge)

Parenting the parents:

(Answer key)

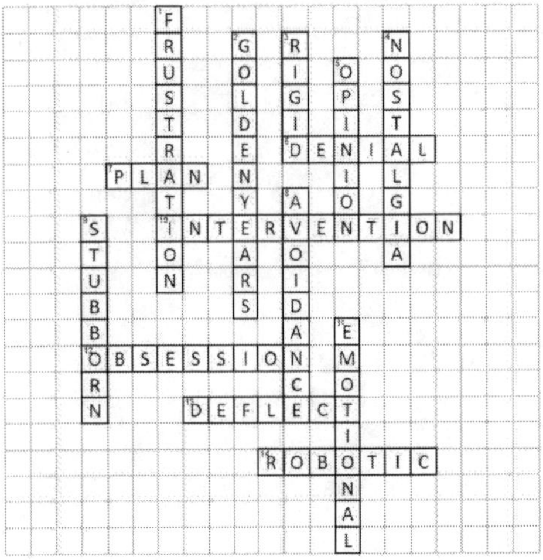

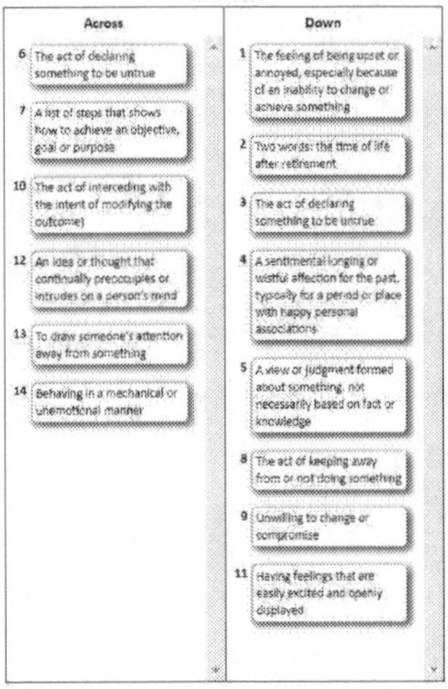

CLUES:

Across

6 The act of declaring something to be untrue

7 A list of steps that shows how to achieve an objective, goal or purpose

10 The act of interceding with the intent of modifying the outcome)

12 An idea or thought that continually preoccupies or intrudes on a person's mind

13 To draw someone's attention away from something

14 Behaving in a mechanical or unemotional manner

Down

1 The feeling of being upset or annoyed, especially because of an inability to change or achieve something

2 Two words: the time of life after retirement

3 The act of declaring something to be untrue

4 A sentimental longing or wistful affection for the past, typically for a period or place with happy personal associations

5 A view or judgment formed about something, not necessarily based on fact or knowledge

8 The act of keeping away from or not doing something

9 Unwilling to change or compromise

11 Having feelings that are easily excited and openly displayed

Chapter 17
Wishbone

when you'd present me with the wishbone
from the chicken you baked
we'd both tug on the upside down "U"
my pinkie finger hooked around one end
your pinkie finger hooked around the other

if I snapped off the larger piece
i'd make my secret wish:
to be picked as narrator for the school play
for my pet hamster to still be alive
for a brother or sister
not until later did I learn that wishbones weren't just for wishes
that they help strengthen a bird and support its chest when it is flying.

in a way the wishbone has done the same for me.
thoughts of our long-ago tradition help me to be strong
now that I must fly without you.

Chapter 18
The Comforter in Chief

Immediate Opening
We are looking for a new addition to our household.

Position: Comforter in Chief
Location: Boston, MA area
Date prepared: Summer 2020
Remote option: No
Visa sponsorship: No
Fulltime: Yes
Vaccinations: Required. To be administered after arrival if necessary
Application deadline: Posted until filled

About Us
Lisa and Alex, a couple that has experienced significant stress since taking their vows, are interested in opening their home to a puppy who can provide emotional support.

Skills required
Easily adaptable to a new environment
Trainable
Friendly

Enjoys car rides
Affectionate and cuddly nature
Responds properly to commands
Enjoys playing chase and fetch
Minimal barker

Salary:
Fiber-rich puppy kibbles from local pet superstore
Continuous supply of fresh water
Cushioned dog bed
Grain-free dog biscuits, gourmet cheese slices and baby carrots

Bonuses:
Based on aptitude for training to do business outdoors and achievement of required skills (see above)
Spa treatments at the grooming salon
Frequent walks at the state park and sheep pasture
Out-of-town car trips
Inclusion in family portraits

If this sounds like you, we hope to hear from you.
ruff@ruffruffbowwow
ruffruffbowwow.net

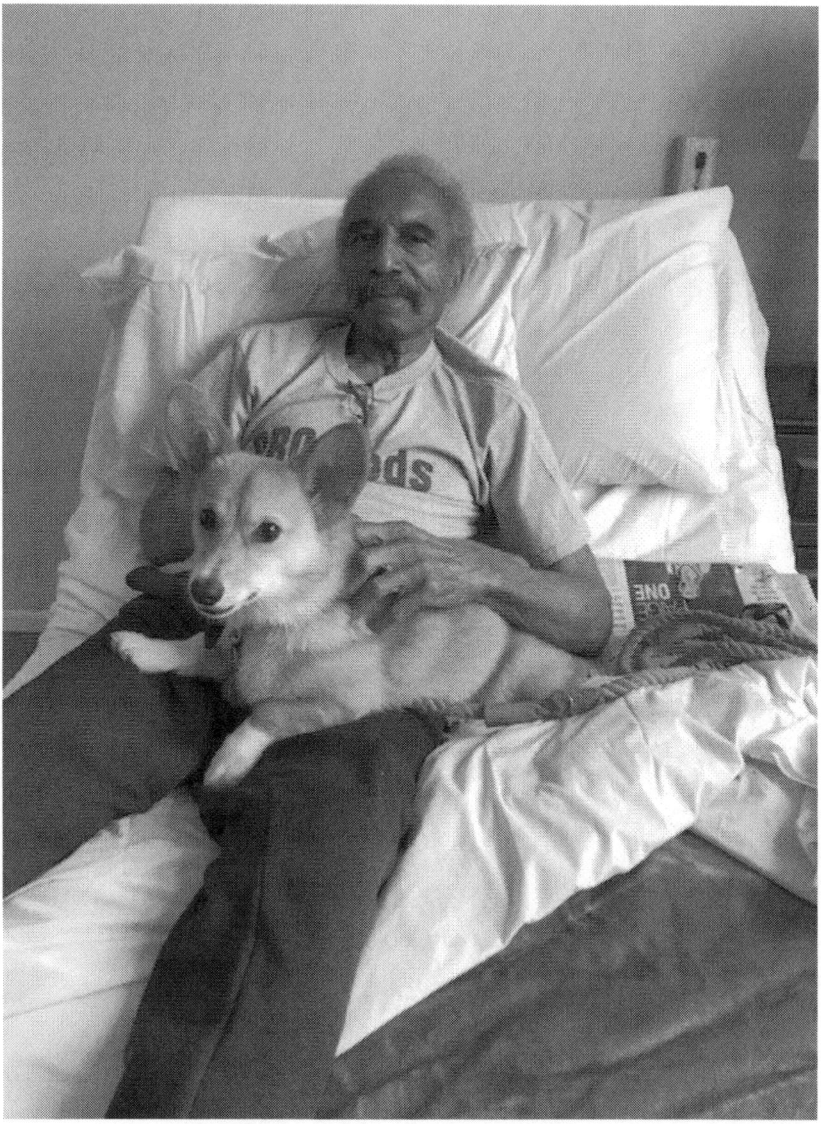

Chapter 19
Annual Evaluation Form

NAME Regina
BREED Pembroke Welsh Corgi
POSITION Comforter in Chief
TYPE OF EVALUATION Annual
EVALUATOR: Lisa

EASILY ADAPTABLE TO NEW ENVIRONMENT

RATING: OUTSTANDING

COMMENTS FROM EVALUATOR: On the day you arrived, you were silent, your eyes were wide and you looked terrified. The driver had to reach into the back of your crate to pull you out. You were eight weeks old, a tiny ball of sandy-colored fur with a lightning bolt marking on the back of your neck.

Those first few weeks were challenging, but that was to be expected as we adjusted to each other. I now understand why you chewed the fabric off the legs of our sofa and loveseat and gnawed on the cord to my laptop until the wire was exposed. You were teething, nervous being in a new environment and likely experiencing anxiety whenever one of us wasn't home with you. Within a few months you stopped chewing our belongings when left on your own. I knew you liked your new home. Within days of your arrival, you'd curl up for a nap just about anywhere and loved to play "chase" with me. The arm of the sofa nearest the window became your "lookout" spot. What a comfort you became!

TRAINABLE

RATING: SATISFACTORY

COMMENTS FROM EVALUATOR: You are a quick learner! Every so often when we couldn't get you out the door in time for your walk and you'd had an accident in the house, we'd wag our finger at you, stomp our feet and take you outside immediately and point at the grass so you'd understand where you should do your business. The training treats we gave you helped with the process.

It only took about three months to train you to "go" outdoors. Once, Alex noticed a strong odor of "BM" and discovered that you had gone behind a chair, not knowing that the smell would give you away.

During these months, I found joy in playing chase with you and carrying you around on my shoulder like a little doll baby.

You are beginning to properly respond to commands, such as "sit" and "stay," but if a neighbor calls to you, you'll dart off and ignore my command to "stay."

FRIENDLY

RATING: OUTSTANDING

COMMENTS FROM EVALUATOR: One of your greatest strengths is your friendliness. You are one of the most popular dogs in our neighborhood, partly by default, because corgis are rare in our neighborhood (and they were Queen Elizabeth's favorite dog) and because of your personality. Whenever I'm walking you and other humans are nearby you put your ears back in a friendly demonstration and pull on your leash like a sled dog to get to them to greet you. Just about everyone in our neighborhood knows your name. People call to you from their cars! You and your canine friends—Max, Roxy and Scruffy—play well together, chasing each other in the backyard, rolling around and flipping over each other. You are assertive during your playfulness, which is an important characteristic to have. The other dogs are much larger than you and play rough sometimes. I've heard you screech loudly to let them know to ease up.

ENJOYS CAR RIDES

RATING: OUTSTANDING

COMMENTS FROM EVALUATOR: I debated whether to bring you with me on the three-hour car ride to Mom and Dad's during Mom's illness, but I needn't have worried. Halfway to Connecticut I pulled you out of the pet taxi in the back seat and let you ride shotgun. What a great companion you were! Standing with your front legs on the dashboard, you seemed fascinated with everything that whizzed past us. Every so often you'd alternate from curling into a ball to take a nap to resting your chin on my arm while my hands were on the steering wheel.

AFFECTIONATE AND CUDDLY NATURE

RATING: OUTSTANDING

COMMENTS FROM EVALUATOR: I tied your leash to the leg of Mom's bed—you tried to gnaw on it but it was a hospital bed with a metal frame, so you gave up—which allowed you to jump and run around in a controlled way. I raised Mom's bed so she could sit up. She smiled watching you play and referred to you as "the baby." Mom got attached to you quickly. Anytime I didn't have you in the room with her, she'd say, "Where's the baby?"

A few days before Mom passed away, when she was no longer conscious, I carried you to her bed. I put you next to her and you repeatedly licked her hand. Mom began muttering. "It's the baby, Mom," I said. "It's the baby kissing you." My love for you deepened watching you comfort Mom.

You have always wanted to sleep near me, poked at my hand with your nose, rolled over on your back to signal that you wanted a tummy rub. All these became especially meaningful for me as I grieved the death of Mom.

After we moved Dad to a memory care community, I'd put you on his lap and he would say "this is a beautiful dog" and pet you while we talked. I have a photo of the two of you, him sitting at a table eating a chicken wing and looking down at you and you sitting at his feet looking up hoping he'd share it with you.

MINIMAL BARKER

RATING: OUTSTANDING

COMMENTS FROM EVALUATOR: You are a naturally quiet dog. The only time you bark is when someone rings the doorbell or other dogs are being walked near our home. I can't recall you barking late at night disturbing our sleep.

ROOM FOR GROWTH

COMMENTS FROM EVALUATOR: We would like for you to respond more consistently to commands, such as "sit" and "stay," and not allow yourself to become distracted and ignore our commands. You have demonstrated a pattern of begging, following us around while we enjoy a snack and at mealtimes. For example, we'd like to be able to have dinner without you hovering under the table or by our chairs, peering up at us, hoping we'll drop a crumb. In the next year, we would like you to significantly curb that behavior.

OVERALL RATING

COMMENTS FROM EVALUATOR: You are receiving an overall rating of "outstanding." You have met all the skills required, helped to reduce the stress we feel and make us laugh every day. Alex and I were a couple. With you here, Regina, our Comforter in Chief, we feel like a family. You are deserving of bonuses. Your spa treatment and photo session for family portraits have been scheduled.

Chapter 20
Statement Of Experience

Entry-level parental caretaker and geriatric case manager successfully managed all Dad's needs through his decline into Alzheimer's and Parkinson's disease using "seat of the pants" style of management. Prepared to advise others taking on similar role.

Researcher | 2019-2022

- In an effort to understand Dad's personality changes and strange decision making, enrolled in an Alzheimer's Association workshop. Jaw dropped while watching the PowerPoint presentation because the behaviors of sufferers cited matched Dad's exactly. Read through packet of support materials and mailed them off to Mom.
- Cornered co-worker in the lunchroom to find out how he managed to keep his elderly father from driving. Decided that unhooking the cables from the car's battery would present too much of a learning curve. Worked on plan with sister, aunt and Mom to hide the keys.

Financial Planner | 2019-2022

- Got Dad to agree to grant me durable power of attorney after he asked for my help trying to organize and pay stacks of bills already paid, dated 2015. Gritted teeth at the attorney's office when Dad refused to check box on his updated Last Will and Testament allowing my sister and me to have control of the family home.
- Lay awake at night upon realizing that very little money was in either Mom or Dad's accounts to pay for Dad's extended care at nursing home following his hospitalization with COVID.
- Convinced nursing home business office manager to release Dad with only a $5,000 down payment on his bill and the remaining $50,000 to be paid at a later date.
- Read through threatening letters mailed from law firm representing nursing home stating that the bill needed to be paid in full immediately.
- Refused to open additional letters from law firm stating that the bill needed to be paid immediately.
- Refused to return phone calls from law firm.
- Sued Dad to get control of family home to pay off the nursing home.
- Sold the house and exhaled because proceeds would keep Dad at an assisted living facility for about 18 months.
- Lay awake during year two of Dad's stay when the facility raised the cost of all services.

Professional Organizer | 2021

- Excavated items from attic storage space of the house including four artificial Christmas trees, crates of record albums, a box of letters Mom and Dad exchanged when they were dating during the Korean War era, and Mom's high school literature book, in which she had written hers and dad's names over a heart with an arrow through it.

- Found Mom's car title, that she claimed Dad had thrown away, inside of her Bible. Filed it away for safekeeping.
- Arranged for an auction to sell off the contents of the house.
- Filled three dumpsters after few items sold in the auction.
- Sold Mom's car to next door neighbor.

Relocation Specialist | 2021-2022

- Virtually toured assisted living facilities and compared prices and services before making a decision.
- Arranged for movers to bring Dad's favorite recliner and the living room couch to his suite on the memory care floor of his new home.

Personal Shopper | 2021-2022

- Enlisted help of aunt to purchase toiletries and other items Dad needed once I learned that assisted living facility—surprising considering how much they charged —didn't supply all of Dad's necessities.
- After aunt moved back "down South" made the 400-mile round trip journey every few months to bring Dad his supplies.
- Later realized that placing orders through Amazon and having them shipped in bulk directly to the facility made more sense.
- Ordered 40-inch Smart TV for Dad so he could watch his favorite shows from his room.
- Mailed two pairs of reading glasses to Dad when he said another resident took his off a table in the community room and laughed at him when he asked for them back.

- When Dad said he lost the two pairs I had sent, shipped him a six-pack of reading glasses.

Diplomat | 2021-2022

- Convinced Dad that the aide giving him his morning medication was not an unsavory character trying to poison him and, therefore, he should not tuck his pills inside his cheek to spit out later.
- Persuaded Dad to not cancel (for the second time) his appointment to be fitted with a new hearing aid after the previous one got lost, by asking an aide to accompany him one floor below to the appointment.

Professional fibber | 2021-2022

- Told Dad that my sister and I did not sell the house out from under him, that he could return home "soon," when he got "better," that we would hire contractors to begin repairs on the house once the weather warmed up and COVID was no longer an issue, and that he could trust me and that I was telling him the truth.

Administrative assistant | 2021-2022

- Promised Dad that I would bring a notebook and pen on my next visit so that I could write down his business plan for his next enterprise.

Party planner | 2021-2022

- Reserved community room at assisted living community to celebrate Dad's 89th and 90th birthdays. Invited family and friends and the mayor, with whom Dad had worked closely when he was a member of city council. Requested

proclamation from the city, which the mayor's aide presented to Dad at the party for his 89th. Decorated room with balloons and streamers. Served Dad's favorite dessert— strawberry-topped New York style cheesecake. Helped him blow out the candles.
- Got help from assisted living community staff to host virtual New Year's Eve party with Dad complete with noisemakers and party hats.

Trouble shooter| 2021-2022

- Tracked down aide to help Dad when he clicked the wrong button on the remote to the Smart TV, which turned the screen to snow and he was unable to return to the channel he was watching.
- Tracked down cousins who lived in the area to help Dad when he clicked the wrong button on the TV remote, which turned the screen to snow and he was unable to return to the channel he was watching.

Negotiator| 2021-2022

- Tried to convince sister to no avail that it was not a good idea to have a phone installed in Dad's suite despite his pleading.
- Days after the phone was installed, fielded calls from facility director in which he implored me to get Dad to stop calling the fire department asking for water and the police department asking for help.
- Promised the facility director I would take care of the matter.
- Got aunt to visit Dad to have a talk with him about the phone.
- Listened quietly as Dad said he wanted a "real" phone, not one that would only work when he called his friends.

Therapist| 2021-2022

- Commiserated with Dad about how wrong it was for the facility's barber to shave off the mustache he'd had since 1951.
- When Dad called on the phone crying because he said he missed Mom, who'd passed away months earlier, I promised I'd visit in a couple of weeks, which seemed to cheer him up. Later, I realized I had a scheduling conflict and got my sister to go in my place.
- Lay awake 15 months into Dad's stay at the facility, worried that the money from the sale of the house would run out, felt relieved weeks later when he passed away, then felt guilty for feeling relieved. Decided it best to suppress all those feelings.

Advocate| 2022

- At Dad's funeral, ripped mayor a new one for not showing up at either of Dad's birthday parties. Let him know how disappointed the family was that he was a "no show." Did not let the mayor off the hook when he explained that he didn't have complete control over his schedule.

Making Strides Gram
MAKING STRIDES Against Breast Cancer
Making Strides Boston
AKA
1,985 likes
MakingStridesBoston Sharing our PASSION so no one walks alone
#BostonStrides #MSABCBoston #MakingStrides

Chapter 21
Making Strides with Every Step

The Charles River Esplanade, a green and flowering oasis in the heart of Boston, is a popular place for cyclists, joggers, in-line skaters and picnickers. But on the crisp Sunday morning in October that I spent there, most visitors were participating in a 5-mile fundraising walk, adorned in an explosion of pink. Men built like linebackers strolled confidently on the esplanade wearing pink tutus over their jeans and hot pink sun visors. A group of women donned shocking pink troll wigs that resembled giant cones of cotton candy. Some walkers were ebullient as they punched at the sky with their pink pom poms. Others playfully flung carnation pink feather boas over their shoulders with attitude. Pink tiaras full of bling were a common sight. I fit right in.

That morning, dressing for the Making Strides Against Breast Cancer walk sponsored by the American Cancer Society, I glanced every so often at the email I'd gotten earlier in the week from the organization. I needed to work up the nerve to follow its directive: "Use the power of pink to raise awareness and money for the American Cancer Society's breast cancer initiative. Don't hold back on your pink attire," it read. "The crazier you look, the better."

Typically I dress conservatively, blacks, browns, and blues being my go-to colors. But I forced myself out of my comfort zone. I left home wearing a salmon pink knit top, fuschia crop pants, a hot pink fanny pack and neon pink high-topped cross trainers. I would have accented the ensemble with pale pink sweat socks if I could have found some.

I'd had a lumpectomy to remove cancerous tissue in June and was now considered a survivor. Mom had surgery the same month for ovarian cancer and was currently undergoing chemotherapy. I told Mom I would participate in the walk to raise money for cancer research and also to support her in her fight.

"But my cancer is different," she'd responded.

"Doesn't matter," I'd said. "I'll be walking for you, Mom, and thinking of you."

Mom's cancer was detected late. Her oncologist categorized it as stage 3C. According to City of Hope Cancer Center, the overall 5-year survival rate for ovarian cancer is 50 percent, but survival rate varies by stage and other factors. According to the National Institutes of Health the five-year relative survival for ovarian cancer is worse for Black women, at 41 percent. Mom's cancer had spread to her lymph nodes and had burst through her colon. Her prognosis was dire.

My mind was heavy as I walked with my sorority sisters and the other 25,000 participants, thoughts ping ponging from Mom's illness to the possibility of my cancer returning as it had for other breast cancer patients I knew. But after a while my worrying dissolved and I became more in tune with the wonder and beauty around me. I became a nature lover on my first Girl Scout camping trip when I was in the 4th grade. Since then, it's been my habit to take walks in parks and wooded areas in whatever community I lived whenever I could find the time. It was restorative.

The explosion of pink wasn't the only burst of color on the walk. I tromped through a confetti of fallen leaves in various shades of yellow, orange, red, purple and brown. I slowed to watch a great blue heron wading along the riverbank, hoping to catch a glimpse of it scanning the water for a fish and spearing it with its long beak. But that was not to be.

After the first mile I reflected on how odd it was for me to take part in a fundraising walk at all. On a fairly regular basis on Sunday mornings I was one of those drivers held up at an intersection by a traffic cop while runners or walkers for some cause crossed in front of me. I'd be annoyed, thinking they were responsible for my being late to church. I'd wish that they would move a little faster, or take another route next time. Now, I was one of them.

Four months before the walk, I was lying face down in an MRI machine for a combination breast MRI/biopsy procedure, my face wet with tears. I was told by the nurses and technicians to try to lie on the table as motionless as possible. A panic button was pressed into my hand for use in case I got claustrophobic in the narrow tube. Earplugs were pressed into my ears to soften the knocking and buzzing noises of the powerful magnets in the machine.

I'd been through an emotionally grueling several months of repeat mammograms and ultrasounds. One doctor stated that my dense breast tissue on one side had her concerned. It was so dense that if something was wrong with me, she wouldn't be able to see it. Another doctor noted that the breast tissue on the right looked different than the tissue on the left, which didn't necessarily mean something was wrong, but she couldn't be sure. An initial MRI was ordered. Two days later, when my primary care doctor called me, I knew something was wrong. Not only were there spots on the right side in the location of the dense breast tissue that had raised concern, she said, but spots were also identified on the left. Her next recommended step was the combination breast MRI/biopsy.

As I lay in the tube of the machine, my thumb caressing the panic button, I prayed. I prayed as hard as I could that it was a false alarm, that I didn't have breast cancer and that my life could return to normal. I prayed to Mom that she could somehow make everything okay. I wished she could be there to hold my hand. Lead me out of this dark wilderness.

A few hours afterward the surgeon met with me in an exam room. "I don't like to give my patients false hope while they're waiting for the pathology report to come in," she said, her voice gentle and soothing. "I'm pretty sure it's cancer."

I felt numb, not believing this was happening to me. I did a split-second cataloging of all the ways I'd tried to remain healthy over the years, the fitness classes at the gym, racquetball, tennis, table tennis, the fruits and vegetables in my daily diet, and never smoking. I thought, "Shouldn't all of that count for something?"

I asked the doctor whether I would need a mastectomy, chemo and radiation. It was a surreal moment, as if I was outside of my body, watching myself ask her those questions. She responded that the cancer was very small, which meant that my treatment could be minimally invasive. But the specialists would be the ones to discuss next steps with me.

I called Mom. She was quiet at first, probably trying to absorb what I had said and working up the strength to respond.

"You're gonna be alright, Lisa. You *will*."

Mom's voice was faint, but her words were like a weighted blanket, curled around me and easing my anxiety. Mom had been right about so many other matters in my life. I told myself she'd be right this time too.

My life moved fast after the pathology report confirmed my diagnosis. Appointments were scheduled with the surgeon, radiation oncologist and medical oncologist. My cancer was Stage 1. Because of the type of cancer I had, chemo would not be necessary. I entered a clinical trial, which concluded that my risk of recurrence would be the same whether I had radiation or not, and chose to forego radiation. I was prescribed an oral medication that I would have to take for five years to block the agents that created the kind of environment in which cancer cells could grow. Remarkably, within a week of my surgery, I was back at work.

I felt a range of emotions during this period of time, deep sadness and grief, despair, and sometimes moments of joy. Along with Mom, my sister, pastor, Bible study partners and friends surrounded me with love and comfort. I was heartbroken that I had breast cancer, but relieved that it was caught early.

As I completed one mile after another on the Cancer Walk, the dollars I raised added up. After mile five I crossed the finish line, wrapped in the warmth of my sorority sisters and the other walkers, my spirits lifted by the simple activity of putting one foot in front of the other. I hoped that my cancer was truly behind me and that Mom would not give up her fight.

Chapter 22
Perfect Life

Mom knew what I needed. As a child, I had many questions she couldn't answer in a way I would understand. I wanted to know why my hair was thick and puffy when my playmate Antoinette had hair that was straight, silky and flat to her head; why my thighs were big and my behind stuck out when Antoinette's and most of the other girls in my kindergarten class had thin thighs and behinds that were flat; why Antoinette got invited to the birthday parties of our playmates who lived on our block, but I never did.

On a bright summer day when I was five, Mom dressed me in one of my favorite shorts sets, took me by the hand and walked me to a white house with green shutters on the next block.

A very tall lady with brown skin answered the door with a smile. She invited us into the den where a little girl wearing eyeglasses, who looked just like her, was sitting on the floor playing with her Barbie dolls. The little girl had puffy hair tied back in a ponytail and bangs.

Holly* invited me to play with Barbie and Ken while her mother made Kool-Aid for us. Mom went back home to give Holly and me time to get to know each other. Holly was tall like her mother, taller than me even though she was almost a year younger. I spent the afternoon fascinated, watching Holly's mother make clothes for Barbie and Ken on her sewing machine, Holly trying them on the dolls and her mother making any needed adjustments.

Soon, I stopped asking my mother the questions she didn't know how to answer in a way that my young mind would understand. They became non-issues.

I'd spend afternoons with Holly, her girl cousins and friends splashing around in the above-ground pool she had in her backyard. Sometimes we'd jump Double Dutch in her driveway or do the Hokey Pokey at the roller-skating rink. During slumber parties in her basement, we'd be up past midnight giggling and having pillow fights.

Sometimes instead of going to the Baptist church with my parents, I'd go with Holly to her African Methodist Episcopal church. It was refreshing to see that Holly paid less attention during the sermons than I did. Her parents allowed her to sit separate from them in the balcony where she would exchange notes with me and make jokes throughout the sermon.

Holly had older siblings: a sister Celeste* and a brother Bennett*, which I thought was really cool because I was an only child at the time.

Bennett wanted to be a musician. Sometimes Holly and I would sit on the couch in the den, our feet not yet touching the floor, and be Bennett's audience as he played scales to practice for his college classes.

Celeste would invite us into her bedroom where she had her portable record player. She'd put on 45's and teach us the latest teenage dances: The Horse, The Swim and the Mashed Potatoes.

Eventually childhood play gave way to long conversations on the phone between Holly and me about the cutest boys in high school and learning the latest dance steps before the Saturday night parties. Holly taught me the fine art of changing out of a turtleneck or T shirt without getting makeup smudges on it.

Later, we flipped through college brochures together. I enrolled at a historically black university in Virginia, 450 miles away. Holly went to a state college 20 minutes from her parents' house. First semester freshman year I spent a weekend with her at her dorm room and a few weeks later invited her to hang out with me and a friend I'd brought home from college for Thanksgiving.

After that, contact with Holly tapered off dramatically. We were moving in different directions. I became entrenched in college life, reveling in being only with other black students for a change as well as in the opportunities for leadership in campus clubs and organizations. I never got a call from Holly and didn't think to get in contact with her.

But years later, after I'd graduated, I grew wistful for her friendship. I longed to see Holly. I missed going to the house with the green shutters. Mom had told me that Holly had gotten engaged. She had become an elementary school teacher, like her mother, and was engaged to marry an assistant principal.

I wanted to share in Holly's excitement. One weekend while visiting my parents I called her. She and her fiancé happened to be at her parents' house at the time. I watched as they came up the street holding hands. I tried to grasp how it must feel to have secure employment, a promising future and to be very much in love. At the time, I was failing at my job at a metropolitan newspaper in Virginia and trying to maintain a relationship I wasn't even sure I wanted to be in with a commitment-phobic guy I'd met at work.

Sitting opposite Holly and her fiancé in my parents' living room, I listened as she laid out the plans for the wedding and reception.

I asked her, "How do you know when you've met the right person, the person you want to marry?"

She gazed lovingly at her fiancé and said, "You just know."

Months later, Mom and Dad got an invitation to the wedding. I was baffled as to why I didn't. My parents and Holly's were cordial but they weren't close. Besides, I was her childhood friend. Didn't that matter? Did Holly not value the close friendship we once had? I complained to Mom. She said Holly probably didn't invite people who lived out of state. But shouldn't I be allowed to decide whether I wanted to take the trip from Virginia back to Connecticut? I was furious with Holly, although she never knew it.

Mom later told me that Holly's fiancé sang to her as she came down the aisle. She and her husband purchased a home in the suburbs and adopted a child. A mutual friend told me that Holly had prepared a lavish feast one Thanksgiving and had a house full of relatives and friends there to celebrate the holiday. I tried to imagine what it would be like to be her, in a secure marriage, raising a child, and living in a home that I owned and could be proud of. Another friend later told me about a conversation she'd had with Holly in which she talked at length about her daughter and the joys of motherhood.

I would think about Holly on return trips home, but I assumed she wouldn't have patience for an old friend who couldn't figure out what she wanted to do with her career, was still single, living in a small apartment and going through pitfalls and disappointments in her relationships. And I continued to feel stung about the wedding snub.

Years went by and after several job changes and relocations to different parts of the country, I became a news anchor/reporter at a cable television station in Connecticut near my hometown and rented an apartment there. Still, I did not contact Holly. Every time I thought of her accomplished personal and professional life, it became progressively embellished in my mind and served to magnify my perceived failures. I knew that I could never face Holly.

Then one evening after I got off the air at the cable station, I drove past Holly's house to pick up my parents to celebrate their wedding anniversary at a restaurant. I noticed a line of cars outside Holly's parents' home. I assumed it was a social gathering. Over the years her parents had had numerous club meetings, dinner parties, birthday parties and cookouts, so it didn't seem unusual to see many cars there. As I drove past the house the front door opened and I saw a guest entering the home hug Holly's mother. Not unusual, I thought. Maybe it was a friend who hadn't seen her in a while.

When I got to my parents' house, Mom was in the bathroom putting on the finishing touches to her makeup. Dad was in the bedroom getting dressed for our outing. I sat at the kitchen table to wait. "I've got some bad news for you," Mom said loudly from the bathroom.

The last thing I wanted to hear was bad news. It was supposed to be an evening for celebrating. I was hoping Mom was making a bad joke, although it would have been out of character for her to do so.

"I hate to have to tell you this, but I have no choice." I heard her snap her makeup compact shut. I started wringing my hands.

She sat down at the kitchen table opposite me and clasped her hands. My heart was pounding in my chest.

"It's Holly."

Thank goodness it's not anyone in our family. So that's why all those cars were in front of her parents' house. Was she injured? If so, hopefully it wasn't too bad.

"She's dead."

What? How could she be dead? She is only 36 years old? Had she been sick? Was she in some kind of accident?

"She committed suicide."

I sat there unable to speak, think or find words. My throat constricted. It was hard to breathe, as if my windpipe was slowly shutting down. I watched what Mom was saying but couldn't absorb her words.

"When the police arrived," Mom continued, "they had no doubt about what Holly had done. There was no question. It was a suicide."

I took a deep breath. "Wh...Why?" I sputtered. "Why would she do that?"

"We don't know," Mom said gently.

"She seemed so happy in her marriage, with her child. Why would she do something like that?" I asked again.

Mom looked at her hands and shook her head.

Because I was a journalist, I was able to easily get a copy of the police report concerning the suicide. I talked to some of Holly's friends and acquaintances to get more information. I was told that Holly's husband was having affairs throughout the years and bragged about it to her. His psychological abuse crushed her. She had a nervous breakdown, tried to commit suicide, but was rushed to the hospital in time to be saved. She got counseling at their church and began seeing a psychiatrist and was put on antidepressants.

Apparently, she wanted to stay in the marriage. I was told that her husband agreed to stay with her for appearance's sake, but months later announced that he was leaving the marriage. That's when she committed suicide.

I was stunned. I thought back to the day that she and her fiancé had come by to see me all those years earlier. I found it impossible to link the joy of that moment with the anguish she had endured for years. I couldn't believe that the little girl whose laughter I could still hear and whose smile I could still see in my childhood memories had found herself trapped in such a deep, dark emotional corridor filled with such pain and hopelessness that the only solution for her was to willingly cause her own death. I didn't understand how her husband, someone who seemed to adore her, could be so cruel.

I became angry with myself. I had been so focused on my insecurities and self-doubts that I refused to reach out to a friend to simply say hello. In my pettiness I held not being invited to her wedding against her. In my immaturity I made the assumption that she had a perfect life, when no one has a perfect life.

Mom and Dad delayed their anniversary dinner that night and the three of us went to Holly's parents' house to pay our respects. Dad spent time consoling Holly's Dad and Mom and I sat with her mother, siblings, and a host of other people whom I hadn't seen since I left home for college. It had been decades since I'd been in their home. The house and furnishings looked much the same as they had when Holly and I were playing with our Barbie dolls. But nothing would be the same. Not for her family and not for me.

I would not have had the power to keep Holly from committing suicide, but we could have had treasured moments into our adult years.

For weeks it would take me hours to fall asleep at night. For years I would think about her every so often and feel sad. Holly was my first close friend to die. It was a jolt to my system.

Eventually I forgave myself. I gave myself permission to be flawed. I shifted my focus from what I didn't do and put my energy toward what I did do: maintain a beautiful friendship with Holly for many years. I learned to respect and value my emotions and feel my grief, which prepared me for losses in the future.

*Names changed for privacy

Chapter 23
Grieving

Guided by the lessons you taught me, I
Rejoice in the person I've become
Independent, ambitious and caring
Even playful at times.
Visions of your love
Inside of my thoughts
Never leave me.
Gentle memories console my heart.

Chapter 24
Rite of Passage

You were such an active pet when you were in my first-grade classroom. You ran on your exercise wheel several times a day. You sucked on the metal straw attached to your water bottle until your cheeks looked like they were going to explode. You grasped lettuce between your paws and chomped on it. Everyone in class gathered around your cage during free time to watch your every move with fascination. At the end of the school year, the teacher asked for a volunteer to take you home. I wanted you. My hand shot up before anyone else's. I couldn't wait to tell Mom when I got home from school. She didn't react the way I thought she would.

"I'll think about it," she said.

"But Mrs. Schmidt said I could have him," I pleaded.

"I'll have to talk to your father about it."

Mom gave me her decision after dinner.

"Okay. You can have the hamster, but you'll have to keep him in the basement."

I told Mom I wanted you to stay in my bedroom with me, on the main floor, not downstairs by yourself in the basement, but Mom said no.

I visited you every morning to feed you before I went to school and every afternoon when I got home, giving you hamster food, lettuce and carrots. I'd stare at you in the cage for hours sometimes and I didn't understand why you wouldn't run on your exercise wheel anymore. Sometimes I'd come down to see you but you were gone. I couldn't figure out how you unlocked your cage door and ran away several times. Dad would always find you in the laundry room in the washing machine hose. You didn't seem happy.

One morning before school when I went into the basement to feed you, you didn't look right. You were stiff, shrunken, reminding me of cardboard, and leaning against the side of the cage. I had never seen anything like that before in a living creature. I ran up the stairs to Mom in the kitchen. She was washing dishes.

"Something's wrong with Hammy," I said.

She said nothing for a moment. Then, "Go get your father."

Dad peered into the cage. "He's dead," he said in his matter-of-fact way.

I grabbed Dad around the legs, pressed my face into his knees and started wailing.

"I noticed last night that he was struggling," he added.

"Why didn't you say something? Why didn't you tell me?" I asked through my tears. In my six-year-old mind I assumed that there was a 24-hour hamster hospital we could have taken you to that would have made you all better.

Mom let me stay home from school that day.

I pulled out the song book that came with my children's electric chord organ and played sad songs on it. I stopped in the middle of a number when Mom emerged from the bedroom during a commercial break from one of her soap operas.

"You never liked Hammy," I spit out at her as she walked past me toward the kitchen. Mom looked hurt, but said nothing.

Later that day I ventured out of the house into the backyard onto my swing set. Mom opened the back door and called to me. "I just talked to your Aunt Dorothy. She said she's sorry that Hammy died."

I felt better. At least someone cared.

Late in the afternoon when Dad got home from work, he and Mom asked me to follow them into the backyard to the shade tree at the edge of our property. Dad carried a shovel and a shoebox. I asked

Mom what was in it. She said it was you. Dad dug a small plot for you under the tree and placed the shoebox in it.

"Do you want to say something to Hammy before your father covers up the box?" Mom asked.

This was a new experience for me, saying final words to something that was dead. I didn't know what to say.

"Good-bye, Hammy," I said finally.

Dad covered you and we went inside to have dinner. I realized that you were happiest when you had a crowd, when my classmates and I gathered around you at school to watch you. You enjoyed performing for an audience, not being alone in a basement.

I also realized that Mom and Dad understood how much I valued you and when you died they understood the opportunity they had to help me with the grieving process by honoring my sadness with the backyard burial. This was my first experience with death, my first experience with grief. Over time I would learn that your death helped me to process future losses.

If I could go back in time to the moment when Mrs. Schmidt was asking for a volunteer to take you home, I would have let one of my classmates have the opportunity. Maybe then you would have been happy.

Chapter 25
Squirrel

People spend good money to rid their homes of squirrels. They'll place an emergency call to their local rodent removal company and pay whatever it takes to come out on the winning end of a rodent invasion.

But in our case, Dad not only welcomed a squirrel into our home, he vowed to cook it!

Ours was a tree squirrel, the kind that lives in woodlands, forests, and backyards, gracefully scampering and leaping from branch to branch like a trapeze artist, squeaking, making nests, and climbing trees backwards and forwards.

But that life was long over for our squirrel.

"Remember when we used to catch these and cook 'em?" my Uncle Norvelle, Dad's brother, said, his voice bouncing off our kitchen walls. He handed Dad the chilled squirrel parts, encased in white plastic, as if it was a prized trophy. The package took the shape of a large sausage.

"Sure do," Dad said, in his typical cool, composed, measured manner. Yet his eyes twinkled as he cradled the package in his palms.

Uncle Norvelle had brought the squirrel with him on one of his rare trips from Virginia to our home in Connecticut. I don't know if he took a train or drove, but he'd managed to keep the rodent cold for the duration of the journey.

Dad found space for the squirrel in the freezer, poured a couple of scotch and club sodas and he and Uncle Norvelle spent the rest of the evening reminiscing about their childhoods in Lowesville, a small farming village west of Charlottesville.

Up until that day, I'd heard nothing of Dad's adventures squirrel hunting with his brothers, but I was not surprised. Dad, the youngest of 13, had often entertained my sister and me on long car trips with details of his many adventures growing up.

Dad's family lived close to a creek. Grasping spear-like metal instruments called gigs, he said he and his brothers would wade into the water and jab frogs with them. Then they'd fry the frogs and make a meal of them.

From the back seat of whatever sporty car Mom and Dad had at the time, Sylvia and I would pull ourselves up to the edge of our seats as Dad described the hunting and capturing process. "What does a frog taste like, Daddy?" we'd ask. "Is it nasty?"

"Not at all," he'd say in his casual way. "It tastes just like chicken."

Dad told us one of his chores before going to school each morning was milking the neighbor's cows. He hated it. His hands would get so sore and tired from squeezing the cow's teats that he came up with an ingenious way to make the job easier. He added water to the milk buckets so that it would appear that he had done all the milking. This seemed to work fine, until one day the neighbor lady said, "Peck (my father's childhood nickname), the milk don't taste right. I cain't (sic) figure out what's wrong with it."

He simply shrugged and feigned ignorance. Mom said she felt sorry for the cow.

Dad played the guitar when he was growing up, strumming tunes while his brothers gambled at card games. He said unbeknownst to his brothers, coins would fall between the floor's wooden planks in the old building where they played. He said one of the benefits of being a small kid was that he could crawl under the building and at the end of the night collect the loose change for himself.

You *are* gonna cook it, right?" Uncle Norvelle asked Dad.

"Sure am" Dad responded.

But as weeks turned into months, the squirrel became a long-term resident of our freezer, front and center surrounded by Swanson TV dinners, meatloaf-sized portions of ground beef wrapped in aluminum foil and A&P brand chicken drumsticks.

I rarely opened the door to the freezer of our early '70s combo refrigerator-freezer during my pre-teen years. Mom did nearly all the thawing and cooking at the time. But on the off-chance that I had a hankering for a popsicle in the months after Uncle Norvelle's visit, I learned to divert my eyes. The plastic encasing the squirrel hugged the contours of its little body parts and left me repulsed.

I don't think that Mom was fond of having wild game in the freezer either.

"Are you gonna cook that thing?" Mom would blast the question at Dad every few weeks, with emphasis on the words, "that thing."

I'd hear Dad respond, but I was never in close-enough proximity to make out what he said. From his tone of voice he didn't sound as enthusiastic as he had during Uncle Norvelle's visit.

Eventually, the squirrel ended up in the back of the freezer, the edges of its plastic casing the only thing visible. And one day I opened the freezer door and the squirrel was gone.

As distasteful as it was—at least to Mom and me—Uncle Norvelle's gift was thoughtful. It opened the door for brothers to bond for an evening, to look back on their carefree childhood days.

I don't think Dad ever had any intention of cooking Uncle Norvelle's gift. His enthusiasm in the moment may have been fed by both graciousness or a desire to not have his brother thinking that he'd forgotten his roots. Maybe both.

Like many nostalgia gifts the squirrel had its place briefly in the present and permanently in the past where it was destined to stay.

Chapter 26
Squirrel Stew

Here's a recipe Dad could have used if he'd decided to cook the squirrel.

Ingredients For Squirrel Stew

1 squirrel, cut up
all purpose flour
salt and pepper
2 1/2 Tbsp butter
7 c boiling water
1 tsp thyme
1 c corn
3 potatoes, cubed
3 medium onions, sliced
2 c tomatoes, canned
1/4 tsp cayenne pepper

How To Make Squirrel Stew

Dredge squirrel pieces in flour, salt, and pepper.
Brown in butter.
Add squirrel and all ingredients except the tomatoes to the boiling water.
Cover and simmer for 1 to 2 hours.
Add the tomatoes and continue to simmer for another hour.

Chapter 27
Tethered

My mother and I didn't talk on the phone as much once email became popular. She'd log onto her home computer and I'd get on my laptop at work. We'd send a flurry of short missives to each other several times a week, and sometimes several times a day, leaving live conversations for the weekend.

I couldn't wait to check my Hotmail account during a coffee break or at lunchtime to find out the latest from Mom, which clique in her social club had infuriated her, the type of evening gown she had purchased for a dance she and Dad planned to attend, what she thought of the latest verbal sparring among the co-hosts on *The View*.

Sometimes cryptic emails would send me into a panic.

Call me when you get a chance.

Had someone died? Was she not feeling well? Was Dad okay?

When I'd finally have a moment to call her, my fears would be allayed when I'd hear the cheerful tone in her voice.

What do you want for Thanksgiving dinner? I'm putting together the menu.

Or

Your father and I are thinking about driving to your sister's. Do you want to come with us?

I doubt if Mom ever heard me let out a heavy breath on my end of the phone.

There were two periods in my life when the volume of our emails picked up dramatically. The first was when I got engaged at the age of 51. I didn't want an extravagant ceremony and was confident I could plan it myself. My experience organizing meetings and conferences for an international nonprofit organization had provided me with plenty of event planning experience. But with each step in creating an elegant and intimate ceremony and reception, I consulted Mom on all major decisions, often by email. While planning my dream day together, I felt closer to her than I had in years.

The second was when my gynecologist advised me to have a hysterectomy because of rapidly growing fibroids that could be cancerous. I thought I would die on the operating table and hardly slept during the months leading up to the surgery. Mom, who'd had a hysterectomy decades earlier when my sister and I were little, sent me an email assuring me that I would be fine.

Mom: *When is the surgery? Your father and I will come up and we'll stay with you while you recover.*

By the time Mom was 80, the flurry of emails we'd send back and forth had slowed to a trickle.

Alarmed, I called her more often. Sometimes her voice sounded weak, or she'd be stifling a whimper. She was in extreme pain, she said, around her abdomen and the doctors were trying to figure out why.

Eventually, a blockage in Mom's intestines was identified. I prayed that it was benign. Because my sister and I lived several states away our Aunt Mae, Mom's sister who lived nearby, took Mom to her increasingly frequent appointments.

But test results from pathology were not the good news I'd been praying for. Mom was diagnosed with late-stage ovarian cancer.

Aunt Mae took Mom to her increasingly frequent appointments. At these appointments, Aunt Mae would ask for permission to record them on her phone, explaining that they were for my sister and me.

Unlike the emails from Mom that I couldn't wait to open all those years earlier, I let the emailed recordings from the appointments pile up in my inbox. The ache in my heart was too heavy to withstand hearing the unfiltered findings of the doctor and my mother's responses in her raspy voice. I wanted to hold onto the hope that with treatment, Mom could have many more years, even though in my heart I knew that the worst was happening.

After the appointments I'd call my aunt on the phone days later, saying the recording must have gotten lost in junk mail. I felt her summarized updates would be easier to handle.

A few weeks after Mom's funeral, I was looking for an email from an old friend and put his name in the search bar. I didn't find any reference to the friend but a long column of emails from Mom popped up. My chest tightening, I slammed my laptop shut. I'm sure some of her old emails had resurfaced in the past, but now that she was gone, they evoked bittersweet feelings. I wanted to curse the internet, for causing me pain. I didn't want an unguarded moment like that to happen again.

I decided to erase Mom's emails from my account. There were hundreds of them, mixed in with thousands of others. I'd type her first and last name in the search bar and delete all those emails. Then I'd type her last name first, her first name by itself and her last name by itself, each time deleting all of those emails. This seemed to work. No more random emails from Mom popped up.

Until three years later.

Searching for an email thread, one of Mom's appeared in my inbox. The date was December 12, 2017, with the subject line: "Update on the house." My finger hovered over the mouse while I tried to decide whether I should delete that one too. I couldn't remember what the email was about.

Curiosity willed me to open it. The email refreshed my memory on how Mom and Dad had been thinking about downsizing to a condo and putting my childhood home—the home they'd lived in for more than 50 years—on the market. Mom stated that a buyer was interested in the house, but backed out because of recent water damage caused by a burst pipe under the street in front of the house.

I scrolled down to read the rest of the thread, my stomach churning like a cement mixer.

Mom: *I will be going into Yale New Haven Health Smilow Cancer*

Hospital on Wednesday. I'm very nervous and saddened about what the outcome will be.

Me: *Why the cancer hospital?*

Mom: *I'm not sure. She (the doctor) seems to think that there is something wrong with my blood.*

Me: *Mom, I pray that there is nothing wrong with your blood. If there is, I wouldn't be able to breathe.*

Mom: Try not to worry about me, Lisa. I will be strong and pray that there is nothing seriously wrong. I want you to live a long and happy life. I will keep your thoughts and prayers in my heart,

Mom

Reading this exchange, I lingered over each word. I felt my mother's worry about her health and the love she expressed, how she wanted me to go on with my life and enjoy it, no matter what happened to her.

I remember how I prayed that night, that I would never have to face life without her. She was 80. I asked God to let her live until she was at least 90.

Instead of hitting "delete," I saved the email. I also let the other emails from Mom I knew were still in various parts of my inbox to stay put along with the recordings from the doctors' appointments. I realized how meaningful those emails were to me. I would not delete any more of them. Whether I decided to revisit them or not, just knowing they were there would help to gently pull me forward in my journey without her.

I continue my email conversations with my mother, my inner guide, my advisor, my champion, not by tapping on the keyboard, but in my mind.

Me: *Thank, you, Mom for the money you left me. I was able to use it to buy my beautiful home.*

Mom: *I'm glad that I was able to help out. All I've ever wanted was for you to be happy.*

Me: *My hair is starting to turn gray. It's sprinkled here and there, just like yours was.*

Mom: (laughs) *I used to pluck my gray hairs, but after a while I said to myself, 'If you keep this up you'll be bald.' You can always put a rinse in it like I did, or leave it like it is. You've always had such beautiful hair.*

Me: *I wear your wedding band on my left hand with my wedding band and your ring on my right hand. When I tap the diamond with my index finger, I'm signaling you to let you know that I'm thinking of you.*

Mom: *I know, my dear. I'm well aware. I'm thinking about you too. All the time. Love you!*

Chapter 28
Helpless

The shot from the pellet gun punched a dime-size hole in Mom and Dad's living room picture window, shattered the glass of a framed photo of me displayed on the upright piano, ricocheted off the frame and nicked the corner of the wall separating the living room from the kitchen.

It was the late 1990s. I was living in Wilkes-Barre, Pennsylvania, working as a TV news reporter. If I hadn't come home for a weekend visit when I did, I probably wouldn't have known about the incident.

Mom greeted me with a broad smile and a hug as I walked through the front door. But when I asked about the window, her face dropped. She didn't want to talk about it. I only managed to get a few details from her.

The shooting occurred weeks before my visit and happened sometime in the middle of the night. Mom and Dad were in the bedroom asleep. They did not call the police. I asked Mom why. She ignored my question.

At the time, Dad was president of the Greater Bridgeport Branch of the NAACP, which was flourishing under his leadership. Fundraising awards banquets held each year drew hundreds to a downtown hotel and featured high-profile speakers—husband and wife actors and civil rights activists Ruby Dee and Ossie Davis, and Anti-Apartheid Catalyst Randall Robinson among them.

Dad spearheaded rallies at city hall to address social injustices. Journalists with the local media sought his perspective on community issues. Aggrieved citizens came by the clothing store to seek his counsel, particularly on racial issues, and get the NAACP to provide legal help. I was proud of Dad. But I also worried about him.

Not long after he was sworn in as branch president, he began to get death threats on the phone and in the mail. Threats were commonly laced with the N-word. Mom said Dad showed her some of the threats that came in the mail. She told him she didn't want to see any more of it. It was too upsetting. She didn't understand how he was able to tolerate it.

"What if" scenarios ran through my mind many times. What if one of them had gotten up that night and walked toward the kitchen as the pellet ripped into the house? What if the shooter showed up again and decided to take more shots? Pellet guns can cause serious injury and have killed people.

Death threats come from hostility, fear and insecurity. The threats were designed to intimidate Dad, to coerce him into ceasing his civil rights efforts. I knew he wouldn't.

Dad never spoke to me about the shooting or the threats and intimidation efforts. I didn't understand why they wouldn't call the police or take measures to make their home secure. I wanted to protect them but felt helpless.

567·269

Chapter 29
A Better Life

On car rides down I-95
When my feet barely crested the edge of the back seat
I asked you why we didn't live Down South
Instead of Up North
We wouldn't be in the car eight hours getting there
To see our kin.

The ones who talked real slow
And said "y'all" and "fixin'" and "flustrated"
And "tarred" when they wanted to get some sleep.
The ones who sat in house dresses on the front porch
Rocking on metal-framed floral-cushioned lawn couches
As they held onto fly swatters they'd forgotten to leave in the kitchen.
Turning their heads until they almost broke
At the sight of an ambulance going by.
Then talking about it all evening
Until the lightning bugs came out.

Lisa Braxton

You held loose onto the steering wheel
Looked at me through the rear-view mirror
Your eyes twinkling and simply told me
“Your mother and I wanted a better life.”

When my feet almost touched the footwell you told me what a better life was—
A place where a white playmate was your best buddy after school
But did not get on his school bus the next morning, threw rocks at you and called you a n_____
As you waited for your bus to your own school
The one with worn books and grades merged in one classroom.

A place where you didn’t have to go to the back door of the restaurant to order a meal.
Where you didn’t have to step off the sidewalk for “Miss Ann” and “Miss Kate” coming in your
direction
And keep your eyes lowered as they passed you.
A world I could not fathom.

Years after my feet reached the brake and gas pedals easily
I took my own car ride
Not venturing Down South
But staying Up North
In my own neighborhood
Got chased by a driver I accidentally cut off.
Got called a n_____,
Practically got run off the road.
Where’s the better life?

NO RETREAT ON CIVIL RIGHTS
NAACP
GREATER BRIDGEPORT, CT. BRANCH

Chapter 30
A Walking Life

On a summer morning I wake to a pewter sky, the howls of coyotes celebrating a kill in the woods behind our home sometime in the night a faint memory replaced by the coo-oo-oo of a mourning dove trying to locate its mate. I roll over to my husband whose snoring reminds me of the rumble of an amusement park Tilt-a-Whirl and whisper in his ear, "I'm taking her to the park." The "her" is our Pembroke Welsh Corgi, Regina, "The Queen's Dog," as her breed is known.

I snap Regina into her harness and lift her 21 pounds over the zippered opening of her pet carrier and maneuver her inside despite her effort to straddle the carrier with her hind legs. She'd rather ride shotgun, front paws on the dashboard, hind legs on the seat, watching scenes of life go by. I cup the back of her head like police do with a criminal they're putting into the back seat of a squad car and zip her in.

She begins to whimper when I turn into the entrance of the nature preserve, apparently recognizing the sound of the car's tires on the different pavement, and the dog-whistle level sounds of her fellow canines padding along the dirt paths.

Sniffing foliage, grass and soil on our walk is intellectual stimulation for her. My experience is different. Taking in the vibrant colors of the foliage and the floral scents emitted as I walk help me relieve stress and relax.

In the early days, on spring days when I was six, walking was about getting the baby some air, the baby that I'd asked for because I wanted a brother or sister. To prepare, Mom would hand me a Wonder Bread bag empty except for heels of bread loaves. She'd instruct me to tear them into small pieces. She would put Sylvia in a onesie and a matching bonnet, put her in the baby carriage and tuck a blanket around her. She'd push the carriage and we'd walk through the neighborhood, the suspension system of the carriage squeaking, the retractable hood protecting Sylvia from the sun. I'd hear the bubbling brook of the pond before I'd see it, its melody filling me with excitement. I'd giggle and clap my hands watching the ducks change direction and paddle toward the bread bits I'd tossed, stabbing them with their beaks for a quick snack.

Eventually, Sylvia will walk to the pond, one hand in mine, the other in Mom's. I show my little sister how to toss bits of bread to the ducks and watch her enjoyment.

Floats, clowns, musical performers, marching bands and fire trucks fill the streets of Bridgeport for the annual Barnum Festival Great Street Parade. I keep in mind what Dad showed me from his military training, how to mark time while marching with my Girl Scout troop to get back in step. I have a tendency to get distracted and get out of sync. After the parade kicks off, I spot Dad and Sylvia along the route. We wave at each other. They continue to pop up at different locations on the parade route and I spot them every time. When I get home, Dad says to me, "You've got eagle eyes."

Our feet were expressive, our voices were not, denying the authorities the power to suppress us. Dad led the Greater Bridgeport Branch of the NAACP in the March on Washington in 1989 with Mom at his side and Sylvia and me right behind them, literally following in their footsteps. Dad and other NAACP presidents across the country had answered the call by Executive Director Benjamin Hooks to participate in a symbolic silent march to protest recent U.S. Supreme Court decisions that Hooks said rolled back progress for women and people of color. We rallied at the National Mall with the thousands and then walked to the U.S. Capitol. Mom frowned at the Capitol building as we approached it, shut her eyes and turned her head away from it in a dramatic silent message to lawmakers.

It is evening. The lights are dimmed in Mom and Dad's room. Mom is in home hospice and Sylvia and I are watching TV with her. Dad slowly makes his way up the hall to the bedroom, Parkinson's disease making his gait precarious, the rattle of his metal cane announcing his arrival.

He peaks around the doorway at Mom. "You need to walk."

Mom picks her head off the pillow slightly and asks him to repeat what he said over the sound of the TV.

"You need to walk," he says louder and more insistently this time. "If you get up and walk, you'll feel better."

"Dad, she can't walk." Sylvia sounds exasperated. "She can't get out of bed. She's weak. She can't walk."

He responds, "Oh", stares at Sylvia for a moment and then awkwardly backs out of the room.

I sit there trying to figure out why his remark sounds familiar. It takes me a few days to remember why. While doing research for a novel involving American slavery, I read a slave narrative in which an enslaved African said that getting out of bed and walking was a remedy for illness. In fact, the woman had said, "You'll feel better if you get up and walk."

I wonder if Dad's enslaved ancestors recommended that course of action in times of sickness and it had been passed down through the generations.

I wake to the sound of cars and trucks zipping down the ramp of the expressway, which runs parallel to the street in front of my childhood home. I check on Mom, relieved that she is still breathing and didn't leave this world while I slept. I feed Regina, put her in her harness and take her to the front yard for her first walk of the day. Dad used to keep the yard in good shape but can't anymore. Now a man down the street cuts the grass for them but that's all.

The yard is Regina's fiefdom. I can tell by the energy in her stride and how she sniffs certain weeds before relieving herself at her favorite spots. My walk with Regina offers me a few moments' diversion from the heartache of knowing that Mom is dying and she will die at any time. I escape into Regina's world, to be in the moment just as she is. I amuse myself watching her roll on her back and beckon me to rub her belly. I refuel and then go back into the house

Chapter 31
The Day Before the Beginning of the End

If I could relive one day in my life it would be the day before the beginning of the end,

relaxing with you on the queen-size bed, me on one side, you on the other,

The *New York Post, New York Daily News* and supermarket circulars between us,

watching *Judge Judy, The People's Court* and the early evening newscasts,

you on the phone fielding calls from friends asking about your Thanksgiving plans the next day,

and you responding that I had arrived home with Alex, and Sylvia and family were on the way.

The day before the beginning of the end, we discussed the menu and the side dishes relatives would bring—

The corn pudding, the macaroni and cheese, the candied yams, the string beans

Whether to use the good plates and silverware, or sturdy plastic ware and the paper plates with the compartments,

How dad vacuumed and dusted and set up the long folding table in the basement from which the food would be served,

And would I drape the tablecloth on the table and arrange the napkins and help carry the food into the basement, leaving the heavy turkey for Alex to carry?

Not only would I want to relive the day before Thanksgiving, 2018, I'd want to freeze it in time.

Because on that day, the beginning of the end, you passed out after the Thanksgiving feast, were rushed to the hospital.

And stayed overnight.

The doctors said you were dehydrated,

Probably hadn't had enough water with your medications.

I was relieved because it was a minor issue

Or so I thought.

Acknowledgement Of Prior Publication

Soothing a Broken Heart
You Might Need to Hear This, February 2022
https://www.youmightneedtohearthis.com/stories/soothing-a-broken-heart
Welcome to the Neighborhood
Solstice Literary Magazine August 4, 2020

Welcome to the Neighborhood - Solstice Literary Magazine (solsticelitmag.org)

The World I Didn't Know Existed
Cognoscenti Dec. 12, 2014
Processing 'Go Back To Where You Came From' When Where You Came From Is Here | Cognoscenti (wbur.org)

Dad's Playlist
Penumbra Literary Magazine Spring 2023
My Biggest Champion *5 Minute Memoir* 2022
Our Messes
New York Times Tiny Love Stories December 2022

Acknowledgments

I want to start by thanking my sister, Sylvia Braxton Lee, who reads many of my essays and stories before they go to publication and provides positive and constructive feedback. Sylvia is the one person who understands how much I miss Mom and Dad. She has been my lifeline.

Thank you to my nieces and nephew, Bryana Reid, Raven Lee and Julian Lee who have always been encouraging. I feel blessed that they are proud of me.

And my goddaughter, Stephanie Harper, a talented writer who celebrates my work.

I am grateful to gifted writer and storyteller Angie Chatman for providing excellent feedback on the works in this memoir in essays.

For choosing *Dancing between the Raindrops* I thank Sea Crow Press Publisher Mary Petiet, who has been a delight to work with. I also thank her for founding Sea Crow Press. Small presses play an important role in the publishing industry. They amplify voices that might not otherwise be heard and need to be supported.

And to my husband, Alexander Reid, thank you for your love and support.

About the Author

Lisa Braxton is the author of the novel, *The Talking Drum*, winner of a 2021 Independent Publisher (IPPY) Book Awards Gold Medal, overall winner of Shelf Unbound book review magazine's 2020 Independently Published Book Award, winner of a 2020 Outstanding Literary Award from the National Association of Black Journalists, and a Finalist for the International Book Awards. She is an Emmy-nominated former television journalist, an essayist, and short story writer. She is on the executive board of the Writers Room of Boston, a writing instructor at Grub Street Boston, and the president of the Greater Boston Section of the National Council of Negro Women. Lisa is a member of the Psi Omega Chapter of Alpha Kappa Alpha Sorority, Inc.

About the Press

Sea Crow Press is an award-winning woman-run independent book publisher based on Cape Cod in Massachusetts committed to amplifying voices that might otherwise go unheard. In a rapidly changing world, we believe the small press plays an essential part in contemporary arts as a community forum, a cultural reservoir, and an agent of change. We are international with a focus on our New England roots. We publish creative nonfiction, literary fiction, and poetry. Our books celebrate our connection to each other and to the natural world with a focus on positive change and great storytelling. We follow a traditional publishing model to create carefully selected and edited books. In turbulent times, we focus on sharing works of beauty that chart a positive course for the future. We welcome emerging writers, experienced authors, and all readers.